Mr. Moffat's Opus

Other books by Stan Moore

MISTER MOFFAT'S HILL
A historical novel, 1904-08 Colorado.
Cam Braun and Mik Mas struggle to run trains over the continental divide's Rollins Pass. A diamond mine scheme comes to their attention and fireworks result.

MISTER MOFFAT'S ROAD
A historical novel about David Moffat's railroad from Denver towards Salt Lake City, set in 1902. Mik Mas and friends help Moffat to overcome unforeseen barriers.

OVER THE DAM
Mik Mas uncovers and works to stop eco-vigilantes in today's Summit County, Colorado.
Fiction (overthedam.com)

SEESAW: HOW NOVEMBER '42 SHAPED THE FUTURE
A fresh look at the crux month of WWII.
Nonfiction (seesaw1942.com)

Mister Moffat's Opus

Stan Moore

This is a work of fiction. Any resemblance to persons living or dead is entirely coincidental. Some of the towns and establishments described do in fact exist. However, I have taken liberties with their descriptions and of locations and geographical features.

© 2018 Stan Moore

All rights reserved. No part of this book may be reproduced or transmitted in any form or by any means, electronic or mechanical, including photocopying, recording, or by an information storage and retrieval system—except by a reviewer who may quote brief passages in a review—without permission in writing from the publisher.

Design by Jack Lenzo

To Charlotte, Lucy and Graham

Contents

Foreword ix
Cam's Sketch Maps xi
Dramatis Personae xv

I	The train emerging…	1
II	Steu Wentz did not…	17
III	Looking back, the month…	33
IV	Reconstruction work was never…	45
V	Charity Hovus knew how…	65
VI	The 1920's were…	79
VII	Building the tunnel was…	99
VIII	In an expensive…	107
IX	Earlier that day Cam…	117
X	Longtime friends, Mik…	123
XI	Chari was thinking…	133
XII	Dale scanned the…	147
XIII	A week or so…	157
XIV	Another messenger, another…	167
XV	The tunnel had been…	177
XVI	Fall's melancholy rhythm…	185
XVII	Across town, others…	193
XVIII	"That didn't go…"	205

Afterword 209
About the Author 211

Foreword

THIS IS A COLORADO TALE. EVENTS SUCH AS THE FLOOD, THE tunnel, and the international and domestic news items are accurately described. Some fictional characters were added to provide texture and context.

The 1920's were gaudy, bloody, triumphant, lucrative, and desperate.

Europe and the Middle East were in chaos. Russia was tearing at itself in civil war. Japan and the western powers were feeding on a China which also suffered vying warlords, famine and destruction. The French were bled white generationally and financially by World War I, having marched millions of men into machine gun fire. The Germans did that too, and suffered political, financial, and moral unrest. The British were broke but wouldn't or couldn't admit it: Their Empire's components were working loose, ready to fly away after the next war.

The United States by and large enjoyed prosperity. New inventions and ideas, mass entertainment, ease of communication, the airplane and autos came to most all Americans. Prohibition put its stamp on society. Many vast, varied civic and transportation projects were undertaken.

From 1921 to 1929, the people of Colorado rebuilt a city and constructed one of the longest and highest railroad tunnels in the world. They, like everyone else, enjoyed and suffered through events out of their control.

As always, where there is money someone will try to acquire it by any means. Financial gimmicks accompanied the booming economy. Ultimately those schemes swamped the nation. The good times of 1929 were overtaken by the sluggish gloom of the 1930's.

Author's note

Hopefully you will find this account enlightening and entertaining. Many have helped with this effort, especially my wife Kiki who advised, critiqued, and supported. Not least, she also created the cover art. Many others contributed but if I start a list I will miss someone. Suffice it to say, they are too numerous to mention. Thank you all!

Any errors, misstatements, or mistakes are mine alone.

—Stan Moore

Cam's Sketch Maps

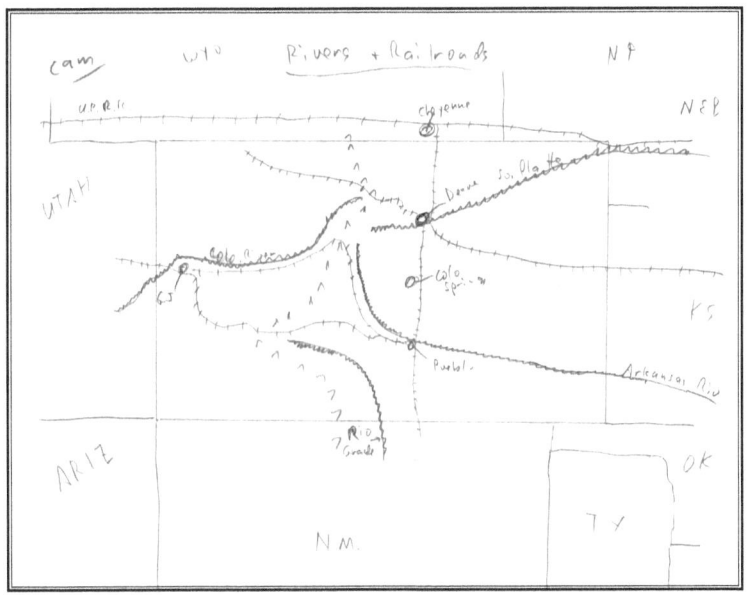

xii | CAM'S SKETCH MAPS

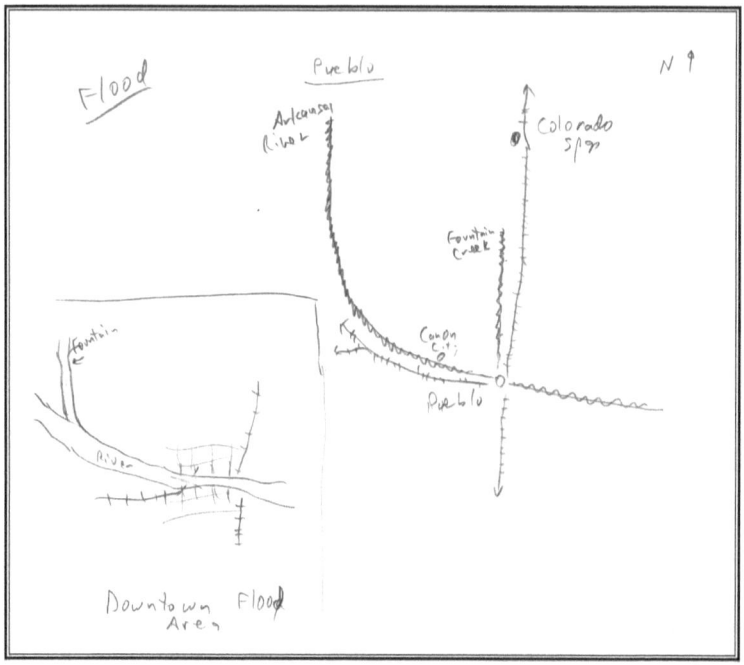

CAM'S SKETCH MAPS | xiii

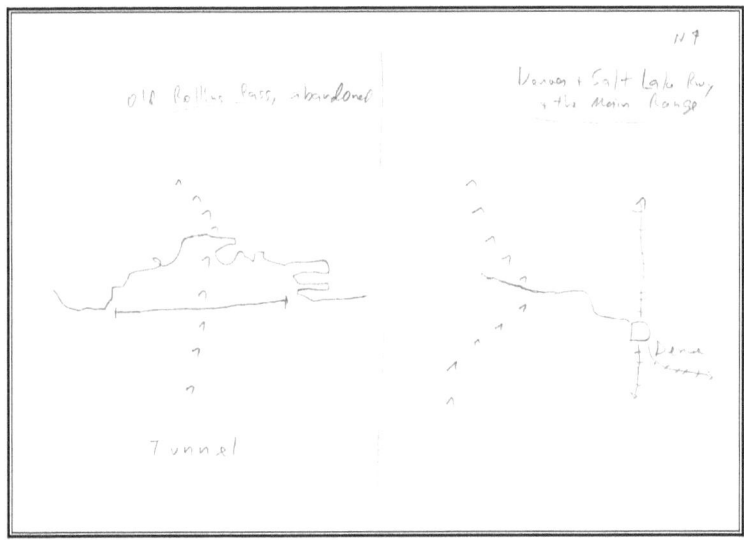

xiv | CAM'S SKETCH MAPS

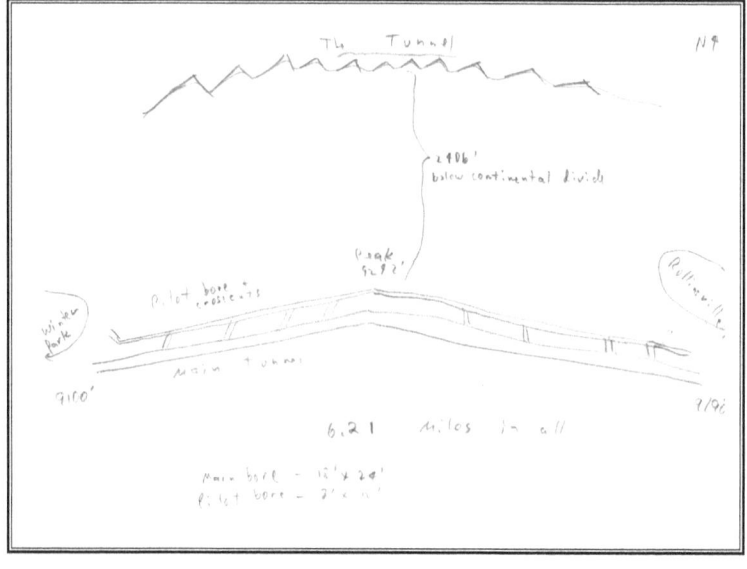

Dramatis Personae

THE CHARACTERS IN THIS STORY ARE FICTIONAL. PEOPLE THAT are noted but not quoted are historical and did in fact contribute to the times. Any resemblance between other fictional characters and any real person or other entity is coincidental and unintended.

Among the main entities and people:

RAILROADS & COMPANIES:
Denver Northwestern & Pacific Railway: Also known as the Moffat Road and the DNP or DNWP. This railroad was founded and built by David Moffat to run from Denver directly to Salt Lake City. It existed from 1902–1913 and ran from Denver as far as Craig, Colorado.

Denver & Salt Lake Railway or DSL: The railroad that emerged from the receivership of the DNW&P in 1913. It also had a life as the Denver and Salt Lake Railroad.

Denver & Rio Grande Railway or D&RG: Railroad formed 1872; one of the main roads in Colorado after 1900. Until 1935 it owned and exploited the only western rail connections in the State.

DRAMATIS PERSONAE

Railroad Routes:

Rollins Pass: highest through railroad in North America, over the continental divide from west of Boulder to Fraser and beyond. It was used from 1904–1928.

Main Range Tunnel, dubbed the Moffat Tunnel: a 6.2 mile tunnel under the divide, a shorter and safer route under Rollins Pass. Opened 1928. To this day it remains one of the highest railroad tunnels in the world.

The Dotsero Cutoff: A short spur which connected the Moffat Road with the D&RG line heading down the Colorado River to points west. This put the Moffat Tunnel on the main route through the State and the nation.

People

Cam Braun Retired senior foreman of D&SL; a consultant on the tunnel.

Mik Mas Cam's friend, a railroad man and lawyer.

Steu Wentz Late operations manager for D&RG in Pueblo; railroad man and friend of Cam.

Joe Eggers Lobbyist, investor, and fixer.

Charity Hovus Financial schemer and dealer in railroad bonds.

Dale Smertz A business man and one of the prime tunnel contractors.

Ella Queue Labor and community activist. Animal rights leader.

Oliver Henry Shoup Governor of Colorado, 1919–1923. Was instrumental in the political compromise which funded Pueblo's recovery and enabled building the Moffat Tunnel.

D. W. Brunton Chair of the Consulting Board of the Moffat Tunnel Commission

George Lewis Tunnel manager and inventor of the 'Lewis Bar,' a mechanism that made the work face safer and more efficient for the rock men digging the tunnel.

Gerald Hughes a water buffalo and player in the Denver Union Water Co as well as the Denver Water Board.

I

THE TRAIN EMERGING FROM THE TUNNEL SYMBOLIZED Colorado's decade of the twenties. February 28, 1928 was a day people waited twenty five years to see.

The locomotive's steam and smoke formed a shimmery veil, pushed through the tunnel by the steel behemoth. The engineer saw it through the glow of the headlight. Being a practical man, he didn't appreciate its beauty and disliked how it cut his field of vision. Suddenly the veil disappeared, pierced as the train burst out of the portal into daylight and escaped the mountain. Huge and grey, the pulsating, hammering machine was greeted by a cheering crowd. All who gathered to see the spectacle were gratified and entertained. The snow on the ground and cold in the air couldn't dampen the mood.

It was a festive occasion. By train, auto, foot and horseback they came. Politicians spoke, vendors sold all sorts of souvenirs and refreshments, reporters took quotes and railroad men watched, satisfied. A few pickpockets worked the crowd. The day was long anticipated and many had it circled red on the calendar. Now it was done, a mere footnote in the histories.

Two friends, old railroad men, reminisced as they rode back to Denver. The Moffat Tunnel carrying a shortened railroad route under the continental divide was now open and working. A watershed event for many, it was especially so for Cam Braun and Mik Mas.

The day was full, truly memorable and special. And long. They left the station from Denver well before dawn and it would be late before they returned. The rocking of the train as it coasted east made the ride doubly sweet. It was a relaxing and soothing sensation at any time. Today, knowing the rails they rode were part of the nationwide ribbon of steel gave an extra glow. Like steel tendons, those rails connected them to the world. The train, led and controlled by its own huge noisy machine, worked its way down the grade back to Denver.

"Cam, where did the years go? It seems like just the other day I started on the crew building the Moffat Road across Eldorado Mountain for Mister Moffat and his railroad. And now here I am, retired for about ten years from the Denver and Salt Lake."

"Yeah. And you go away and come back to town all the time. You disappear for a month or two at a stretch. Where do you go anyway?"

Mik just grinned. "You wouldn't believe me if I told you, Cam."

"Probably not." He too couldn't believe the years had trickled by. "Just think of all those years we spent building over Rollins Pass. Simply building a road over it was one heck of an accomplishment. Then running trains over it, regular as we could, through godawful weather, rock fall, lightning storms…. We spent years doing that for Moffat. And others. Good times, no?"

"Most of them, yes. Some not so good. We recovered too many bodies out of derailed or snowslide accidents." Mik tried to erase images from his mind. He knew he would likely have dreams now that unpleasant memories were recalled by this conversation. The two usually tiptoed around talk of broken bodies and wrecked machines.

Cam was not ready to leave the memories. "Yes, that is sadly true. But all in all, it was good. And here I am, retired from operations manager for a major line." An expression of disbelief and amazement came over him.

"Over the years I worked for just three roads. Started with the old D&RG, the Denver and Rio Grande Western, back before it was known as 'the Dangerous and Rapidly Getting Worse.'" He grinned and continued.

"For a while there it really was getting worse. It got turned around, improved its performance and all. Now it controls much of the Colorado rail traffic, and has for years. All of its western traffic goes through its Pueblo yards, at least for now. The tunnel will change that I'm sure."

Cam tootled on. Mik knew about Cam's background, but didn't interrupt. "After that I went to work for Mister Moffat. Construction foreman on the Denver Northwestern and Pacific, the Moffat Road. I drove the first spike myself! That's where I met you. I stayed there even when the DNWP went into receivership."

Mik had walked down this memory lane with many people, and he again went along on the trip. "Yup. The same road and locomotives and cars and crews were there all along. The Denver Northwestern just plain ran out of money. Something had to be done. The reorganized outfit was the Denver & Salt Lake Railway. Same road, same equipment, new name. Pretty much the same results after a while."

Nodding, Cam brought his life up to his retirement. "And I stayed there for years. A guy who started as a gofer, an errand boy for the Rio Grande ended up as operations manager for a competing line." He smiled wanly.

"It was a fantastic career. I can't believe someone paid me for it. Heck, I got to spend time in the mountains and be around engines and ride trains and set off dynamite. Plus be part of some of the greatest construction efforts in Colorado history. And it was great to do it all with good, honest, hardworking people."

Memories of individual faces and quirky habits, storms, train trips, tunnels, dynamite adventures, and helping people rushed at him. For a moment he was silent. Mik watched, having a good idea the impressions Cam was remembering. He himself had many similar ones. As Cam enjoyed his reverie, Mik spoke.

"So here we are, just celebrating the tunnel's opening. The long dreamed of and talked about tunnel. This is a bittersweet day. Especially for us. We built the road, staking out the grade and laying tracks up over Rollins Pass and all. When we put those rails down we thought it was a short term thing. That road that was intended to be temporary. Moffat and his engineers intended it to be used for only two or three years. They thought that is all the time needed to put the tunnel through. That was in 1904. Almost a quarter of a century ago! Damn! That makes me feel old!"

Neither spoke for a moment, then Mik put the thought they shared into words. "Now that twenty six mile stretch of heaven and hell is finally obsolete."

"Yeah, well the tunnel won't be heaven and hell. It is just a big long dark wormhole through the mountain. But it really will be much better. Safer, quicker, efficient, dry, more profitable."

Cam then switched topics. He loved to spread industry gossip. "The Tunnel Commission has gotten shortchanged. Already! I guess the Denver and Salt Lake has been running freight trains—unofficially and at no charge or expense—through the tunnel. I hear they've been doing it for almost two weeks, since the thirteenth."

Mik took several gulps of his now lukewarm coffee. "No kidding? 'Unofficially,' huh? How did they manage that?"

"I guess all the passenger runs continued up and over the Pass. They were full of folks wanting to say they took the last run over before the tunnel made the pass obsolete. There was some publicity about that and people swarmed to buy tickets. So that probably served as a smokescreen. Everyone had their eye on the passenger cars and trains. Few noticed the absence of freight cars up there. Those that did probably just looked the other way. I doubt the Denver & Salt Lake had approval from anyone. They probably saw the opportunity and just did it."

"What's the old saying, 'better to ask forgiveness than beg permission'? That rule has saved me time and effort more than once."

"True, Mik. As of today, the D & SL took possession in front of God and everyone. From now on they have all the responsibility, expenses and revenues, and headaches. Now others will try to pull a fast one on them. They'll be busy enforcing the rules as well as running a railroad, instead of sliding by."

"Putting the tunnel through was a long time coming, wasn't it? Old Mister Moffat must be smiling down right now. He used up all his fortune to get the road through the mountains. It cost all of his ten or twelve million dollars plus his health. But the man never did live to see his tunnel. Who knew it would take seventeen years after he died?"

"Yeah." Cam held up his hand, four fingers up, and counted them off. "First, the New York and European financial markets wouldn't help him build his railroad. They agreed to fund him then pulled the rug from under him. He uses his own money, but runs out about 1910, gets his friends to put up a little, gets the line a bit further, almost to Craig. Two, he dies in 1911. Three, the Road goes into bankruptcy in 1913. Four, the Pueblo flood."

Mik held up his hand, all fingers splayed out. "And five. The state steps in and helps to finance the tunnel in exchange for also financing Pueblo's rebuilding and recovery." He thought a moment. "Maybe that is backward. The state stepped in to finance Pueblo's recovery, and in exchange the southern Colorado Legislators agreed to a side deal allowing the financing of the tunnel."

Cam nodded. "Rollins Pass 1904, bankruptcy 1913, flood 1921, tunnel 1928. Onward and upward."

The train chuntered down the tracks towards Denver. The two friends fell into silence, reliving the day and their memories.

IN ANOTHER CAR OF THE SAME TRAIN, A MAN AND WOMAN talked. They too relived the day and reminisced about how they got there. Their paths were entirely different from that of the railroad men.

"You didn't get to speak, Dale. That is wrong. Your company made a big contribution to building the tunnel, on the west end. Your crews were the first to hole through when the two ends got close. You should have had a spot on the speakers' platform."

"I know, Ella. That is alright. I'm not an orator as you know. I'd rather be doing than bragging or describing. The tunnel job treated us well and I am proud of what the men accomplished. Of course we didn't do it all by any means. We faced some tough conditions but overcame them, and you are right, we holed through first when the two ends met. I am content with my contributions and don't care if some don't know them. The tunnel is statement enough."

This was a long talk from Dale. Ella admired his work and really thought he should get some credit.

"Still, you should be recognized. Without your company and your leadership and your work, we wouldn't be here celebrating today."

"Yes, E, that's probably true. But I don't need recognition from strangers. I have it from you and others who matter. You and I have come a long way haven't we?"

"From Saint Louis, you mean?"

"Yes. From when we left Denver in a hurry twenty or more years ago. I went ahead and you came to meet me."

"After I got out of jail, you mean. Yeah, I came to find you. I've never told you this, but I wasn't entirely sure that you would be there. All I knew is that you left town and I hoped we would meet at our agreed spot. I mean, I was just out of jail and my life had completely collapsed. And you were nowhere to be found around Denver."

He looked at her fondly. "We had that long held agreement. 'If thing go bad, get out of town and we'll meet on the wharf in St Louis,' was our pact going back forever. We even chose certain days of the week to meet."

"True. It is easy to say when things are going well. When the wheels come off, it is hard to remember and have faith that things will work out."

"I guess so. Anyway, thank God you warned me back then. That gave me the time to get away. And, with the money we had, we were able to get established. And we returned to Denver in style, what, ten years ago."

"Yes. We got here in time for the Armistice and the flu epidemic. It was two or three years before the Pueblo flood."

"Ah yes, the flood. What a God awful mess that was. Enormous destruction and hundreds of people dead. I am glad we were able to go and help them sort things out, start recovery."

"And I have nightmares to this day about the animals. They were everywhere. Strays roamed the streets, dogs, cats, horses, you name it." She shuddered. "Dogs were feeding on whatever they could find. And there were dead horses piled up like firewood, left by the flood waters. It was terrible."

Dale didn't have nightmares about the flood, at least not any more. But he did have vivid memories and occasional dreams of leaving Denver. In a hurry. Looking over his shoulder the whole time.

His mind wandered. With a faint smile he thought of how he had lammed out of town: First he stumbled into a financial windfall. Finding a suitcase full of money, he was awestruck and a bit afraid. The money, he was sure, was sheared from investors in a mine scheme. Actually, he was part of the scheme. He had gone into and promoted it in good faith. At the last minute it came out—Ella found out and got word to him—that it was a scam. She also learned and sent word that he and she were to be the fall guys.

At that point, just who really owned the suitcase and contents was, well, open for discussion. Or interpretation. Or debate. He didn't ask questions or worry about the finer points. Dale just took the money in the suitcase for his own. And he caught an eastbound train in a hurry.

St Louis, Missouri was the emergency site to meet up with his partner. Extricating herself from jail and the surrounding publicity took Ella a while. She managed it and found her way east, and at last she did show up. He faithfully checked their rendezvous every odd numbered Monday and Thursday, as agreed. One day, there she was!

In the meantime Dale invested in a business which owned pieces of other businesses. Ultimately he bought out the other owners. Then he changed the company's name. This was on the ownership papers only. Trade was done under other names, as needed. He and Ella were the partners. The new name was Top Karat Partners. Unusual, but it had a distinctive ring. Known only to the two owners, its seed money came from the mine scheme. The purported mine was named the Karat Top. They had good reason to keep the name under wraps.

Back then, twenty or more years ago, business was good. They worked throughout that part of America west of the Mississippi River. Opportunities were plenty there, limited only by people's blindfolds and prejudices. At first it was not easy for the two. Ownership was new for them and called for a new and foreign attitude.

Ella broke in on his thoughts. He was suddenly back on a train in 1928, celebrating the opening of the Moffat Tunnel. She asked, "Your work on the tunnel is about done, Dale. Now what?"

He chuckled. "E, you do cut to the chase, don't you? You ask a good question, one I am just starting to wrestle with. Now that the tunnel is done, my construction crews will likely be moving on. I'll make no effort to keep them. The construction game is a never ending challenge and I'm tired. Maybe I'll take it easy for a while, rest on my laurels as it were. "

"Not a bad idea, Dale. You have earned some leisure time."

"Who knows, maybe it is time for me to find another line of work. I do know that jumping into another big construction project doesn't hold much appeal. Not that I know of any at this point."

Ella frowned. "Speaking of big projects. I have heard rumors. Not sure who is behind them and maybe they're just talk. But word is a dam may be built. To block the Colorado River. That river is big and any dam would have to be huge! I guess they're talking about putting it somewhere near the little town of Las Vegas in southern Nevada. I can't figure out why they would need a dam there."

"Now that would be a project." He mused a moment. "You know, I was reading about how Herbert Hoover got the western states to sit down and talk a few years back. He was a Cabinet member then, not President. Anyway, there was big hoohah about it in the papers. They treated it almost like he persuaded warring parties to sit down and palaver. Anyway, he got them to agree on how to divvy up the water in the Colorado River. It was announced like the Treaty of Versailles or something. As I remember, it was called 'the Colorado River Compact.' Maybe the dam you mention is part of that agreement."

She nodded. "Now that you mention it, I recall that too. California tried to throw its weight around, I remember reading. The other states banded against it and each one got something out of it."

He was mildly interested. "If there is talk of a dam, maybe there is money to be made. Let me know if you hear more about that, would you?" But for now, I think I am out of the construction business."

Enough water talk. He went back to memory lane, back to twenty years back. Which led to, how they got to be here today. "How did we get into it, anyway? Construction, that is? I left Denver with that money and you joined me."

"Yeah, but like I said, I had to get out of jail first. Then deal with the assault charge old Joe Eggers tried to press on me. I threatened to counter charge and go public. All charges and accusations were dropped." She grinned at that.

The grin changed to grimace. "His sidekick Charity Hovus came around after a day or so. She bailed him out. It seemed like right away, before I got out. She wanted to press charges and I made the same deal—if you do, I go public and press counter charges. That made them think, and like I say, drop the idea. The Sheriff let me out a day later as I recall. It was only three or four days, but it sure seemed like months at the time."

He was listening but said nothing. She went on.

"It was a good thing, Dale. I mean that you made me set aside a little money in a safe place. With it, I was able to buy a one way ticket in the hard seat section. Thank God I didn't have to post bail; that would have used my funds up. The sheriff just released me and I made for the train station. The ride across Kansas and Missouri was uncomfortable. Still, I was real glad to get out of Denver. And it was a truly welcome sight to see you there along the wharf in St Louis. So, to answer your question, we just started working and here we are."

"Yup, Ella, I was glad to see you too. I've never told you. Like you were concerned about me, I wasn't entirely sure you would show up. I had faith in you, don't get me wrong. But things were chaotic then. I knew there was trouble in Denver and didn't know where you were. I had no idea what had happened to you and if you would even want to be with me. I just didn't know what had gone on."

He looked over fondly. "We have come a long way. After we came back to Denver and got set up, we did some recovery work around the Pueblo flood. Then I made contact with some of the old railroad folks we used to cross swords with. Those two events, the flood and the railroad guys, led to the tunnel work."

"Yes, I know. You even hired two of the men who gave us some grief back in the old days. Old Steu Wentz and Cam Braun. And their friend Mik hung around some too. Mik Moss or Mash or something. Anyway, I wasn't too sure about that. Getting used to them didn't come easy. Coming around to that took me a long time as a woman, an animal rights and labor rights fighter. They're actually not so bad, pretty nice really."

She smiled. "I remember once when Steu ran you and me off a work site. Long, long time ago. 1902 or 1903, not sure. Long time. It was on the new Moffat grade above Eldorado

Springs, no rails laid yet, just the grade. Someone had a shotgun and it wasn't us. But it didn't get used, just the threat was enough to make us leave. There was no love lost that day!"

"No there wasn't. He and I have chuckled about it. Now, we can laugh. Everyone was just doing their job." He smiled wanly, thinking about looking down the barrel of that shotgun. It looked big and dark and even the memory was scary. It was very persuasive.

He came back from reminiscing, and answered her.

"But back to your question, Ella, about what's next. I don't know what we'll do now. If you have any ideas or hear of opportunities, let's talk. It is 1928 and the stock market is a good place to invest our profits. There is money to be made."

"Dale, do you think the stock market is safe? It can't go up for ever. Maybe we need to think of some other way."

"Can't hurt to diversify. Let's keep our eyes open." They lapsed into silence.

Dale's thoughts returned to Ella, and started again down the lane of memories, about how they came back to Denver ten or so years ago. Now he remembered another train ride, when they returned to Denver in 1917. That ride had been as fun and relaxing as today's special up to the Tunnel opening and dedication.

His idea, a hope really, was that Ella would ease up on her passions, animals and labor. Not to be. She never relaxed, never softened. Finally he just accepted it all. Her caring about animals and workers actually was good for his business, he found. She could spot weaknesses which gave him leverage. Plus, she was well connected in a part of town he wasn't.

The conversation they were discussing was over ten years back. Even so he recalled it as clear as if it was yesterday.

"Let's get settled into a place somewhere near Denver. Once we have done that, we can find more opportunities. I think between railroads, mining, and agriculture, I will be busy. You will no doubt jump into your causes."

She nodded. Unusual for her, she said nothing.

He made a suggestion, hoping she might pursue it.

"Say, it occurred to me that many tuberculosis patients are coming to this part of the country. Those people have needs and many have money. Do you want to look at building a sanatorium? Or hire doctors and nurses to treat this influx of well off refugees?"

"Maybe. Let's get settled in first. About your sanatorium—I don't know. It may be something needed that we could do. Let me think on it"

This led her off on a toot. "Say, do you think animals get the TB? Many horses and dogs and cats may be suffering silently. I'll have to talk to an animal doctor about that."

Her eyes were pointed west as the train approached the mountains and city. But she was not seeing them, rather was lost in memories. "I wonder if any of the people we knew are still around." It had been years.

"My contacts tell me that those two railroad men are around. Cam Braun will be retiring from the Denver and Salt Lake soon, I understand. Or maybe he has already. I'm not sure about his friend Mik. Can't remember his last name—Massey? Mast? Mann?—anyway those two are apparently still in circulation."

"That's alright with me. We seldom crossed paths even then, and we sure won't now. They were mid level railroad man, not financiers or owners. And that is who you deal with now, Dale. Not workaday men."

"True. Any railroad men we do business with will be well above their level."

"What about Joe Eggers and Charity Hovus?" The edge to her voice said she remembered them, oh yes she did. For a time she was angry at them. But she finally saw that what they did really ended up as a favor to her and Dale. "Who cares where Joe and Charity are? We are better off for them and their antics."

Dale then firmly turned the conversation. "Do you want a home on Seventh Avenue by the Governor's Mansion, or an estate outside of town? There's a lake west of town, out in the country. Sloan Lake, it is called. I'd prefer that. You could keep horses. And have a garden and chickens. If we get some land, you could have more livestock."

"I agree. Having animals would be nice. And, I just think it would be good to be out and away from the city a ways."

The train pulled into the station and the couple put away thoughts of ten and twenty years ago. The tunnel was done and it was time for new adventures!

II

Steu Wentz did not attend the opening. He stayed in Denver that last day of February, 1928. Plenty of trains had steamed through his life. Seeing the first official run through the tunnel held no interest. Trains and the road over the Hill (railroaders' term for Rollins Pass) were a large part of his career. He had helped build and then run the road for years. Hearing 'Rollins Pass' or 'Corona Station' brought memories of snowstorms, smoke filled rooms, derailments, and the camaraderie of making a huge complicated enterprise work and work well. He would often retreat to those memories, high points in his life.

As to the tunnel and Rollins Pass, he was of mixed mind. It was silly but he felt like something valuable and important was being thrown down, abandoned. He like many had poured his life into those switchbacks and tunnels and trestles and water towers and the whole complex web of machines and people. Sure, intellectually he knew the tunnel was better, safer, more efficient, and easier. But still there was hurt in his heart. Never again would passengers share the adventure of riding the highest through train route in North America.

He shook his head, clearing it of such soft, useless ideas. Of course, like all progress and improvements, the tunnel would be good. Everyone would benefit. Passengers riding out of Denver and the entire northwest part of the State would benefit most. At least that is what he figured.

His friends Mik and Cam were just back from the big day. Steu wanted to get their impressions first hand so had arranged to meet them for dinner.

He stood when they came in. "How was the opening? After we spent all those years running trains over the Hill it must have been something to see a locomotive come out of the tunnel! In a way I'm sorry I missed it."

Cam was enthusiastic. "Yes, it was something, Steu. That engine pushed a puff of steam and smoke out ahead of it and it was a grand, dramatic entrance." They shook hands around then sat.

Cam hungrily grabbed a menu. "I'm famished. What's good here?" Steu knew that was just talk. Cam always asked that even though he didn't really care what others liked or might order.

Mik glanced at the menu then tossed it down. "So Steu, how was your day in town? I know you loved the road over the continental divide. This really was something today. And the crowd loved it! The press and everyone was there. I saw a radio crew, broadcasting live. Also saw that a newsreel camera was set up for the shot. Bet they got a good one of the train bursting out of the mountain. You know, the engineer drove through from near Fraser in about twenty five minutes. Twenty five minutes to come from the west side! In the old days that would have taken eight hours! And that was on a good day!"

Steu nodded. "I know. Still, there's something about conquering the range…."

"Romantic bushwah, Steu. The folks in the crowd up there today would certainly disagree. They cheered and jumped up and down when the train emerged. They may have made more noise than the engine!"

He picked up a menu, glanced at the special, and tossed it down again. "I'll have the special," he said to no one in particular. Then he got back on topic. "And all because of a flood in Pueblo."

Steu looked over the top of the menu at Mik. "The political deal and the State getting into the tunnel financing business, yes. And how that put paid to Pueblo's dominance of train traffic in the region. Or I guess it will do that pretty soon. Life takes funny turns, no?"

Cam put his index finger on the menu item he wanted, holding the paper firmly on the table. "I remember hearing about that flood. It was the first week of June back in '21. I came down and sat for the breakfast my wife always made me. We splurged and paid for The Rocky Mountain News to be delivered to our door every day. The paper was already on the table and so I picked it up as I dug in." He looked away into the distance, recalling the day.

"I remember saying, 'Wow, look at this headline! Flood in Pueblo!' I told her, it said '201 Bodies Found, Scores Lost, Pueblo Death Total 500 to 1500.' I will never forget that. The wife almost burst into tears. I have to admit, the thought of all that hurt and damage was awful. And the expense of putting lives back together...."

The waitress, their favorite one, came by. "Are you old gandy dancers ready?" This with a smile, an old inside joke.

The three ordered up, Cam last. He had a special request as usual. "And put some green chilis alongside my steak. The hotter the better."

Her eyebrows went up at this. Cam seldom surprised her. He explained. "My taste buds are feeling worn out today.

Do whatever you can to give them a jolt." She smiled at this and made a note for the chef to douse the steak with hot sauce as well.

Cam went back to recalling the morning of the flood. He looked at Steu.

"I was darn glad that you got out of town ahead of the storm, or so I thought. I was wrong. You were still there. At the time I thought you were up here in Denver, safe. Little did I know. I believed you were out of there by then."

"Yeah, it was this close." Steu held up his hand, thumb and forefinger almost touching. "My last day as manager of the Rio Grande's Pueblo yard was end of May, the thirty first. I stuck around a few days. You know, tying things up for the new guy. Made myself available to answer questions. Say goodbye to old friends, tip one last drink and all. Actually, the plan was for me to jump on the next morning's train. My ticket was bought and bags packed. Ready to come back to Denver. I had already sent my wife and kids out thank God." His expression showed his gratitude. "Anyway, the waters came and I didn't make it out."

The meals arrived and they dug in.

Mik spooned his soup carefully. "It must have been something."

"This experience was confusing and frightful, what weathering a tornado or combat must be like. It is an experience that is impossible to describe or understand unless you've been there. It was, well, it was terrible and ugly. It made me realize how small and vulnerable we all are. And it was awe inspiring how people rose to the occasion and hideous how some people robbed and looted."

He paused, unable for a moment to process the memories. His voice caught with emotion as he started again.

"The rain, my God the rain. Early June is damp, you expect that. But the storm had actually started the previous afternoon or maybe before, on the second or third. I don't remember. So much rain fell that the soil was simply saturated. The ground just plain could not absorb any more." He looked at his friends, making sure they understood.

"That was the case all over the Pueblo area, up and down the Arkansas River valley. Then, insult to injury, even more rain fell in a small area upstream of town. It was near Fountain Creek, the one that runs from Colorado Springs. That storm was a real frog drownder, three or four inches over forty five minutes, something over the top like that. That would be bad in itself, but added to several days of soaking and drenching, it was too much. The land just couldn't handle it, couldn't take it."

He giggled then laughed so hard he almost doubled over. "They say when it rains it pours, right?"

Mik glanced at Cam, shrugged, and clapped a now silent Steu on the shoulder. "Its alright, friend. I know you saw and felt things no one should have to experience. Things you can't really put to words." They waited.

Steu wiped his eyes. "Sorry about that. It is just hard to relive. Plus I wonder why did I come through when the man or woman just down the way died? Why me? Sometimes I feel guilty to be here."

"Take your time."

"So then a wall of water came through downtown Pueblo, past tall buildings and train tracks and all. The wall came along straight down the channel of Arkansas. It was ten or twelve feet high, not exactly sure. But it was bigger than me. The sound was awful. It was kind of a throaty rumble, taking all before it. It rolled like a beach wave and you could see it carrying people, animals, wagons, railroad cars and ties, dirt, trees….truly terrible. After the first wave came through it got quiet. Or quieter. The rumble subsided but it was not silent by a long shot."

Cam stuffed a pepper in his mouth. Mik expected to see smoke coming out his ears, but no. He chewed for a moment, clearly enjoying the taste. Around the mouthful, he asked, "What did it look like then?"

"It was dark and still raining. Couldn't really see except for the fires that broke out. And cries of people, people trapped or people looking for someone or people just screaming, out of their minds, in shock and fear. The next morning, though, with daylight, was a scene from hell. Great God, may I never see such a thing again."

Mik quietly spoke. "Up here, we didn't know how it was. Every rail line to the city was cut. Telegraph and telephone lines were apparently down, but we didn't know that. From the few accounts we did have, we knew there was real trouble."

"There was that." Steu still had nightmares, six and a half years later. This was really the first time he had talked about it. The memories came like the flood itself, going where they would, not controllable. He couldn't stop and just kept talking. At some level he was astonished at the memories, at another level he was relieved to share the burden.

"The day before, there was a railroad depot, and a switching yard, and stores and people and all the things you take for granted in the prosperous rail center of a thriving town. That morning, in Pueblo, I looked out at horrific, almost unimaginable devastation.

He paused, unforgettable scenes tumbling to the forefront of his mind. "Banks of mud were laid down. Pools of water lapped at the curb. Rail cars—box cars, passenger cars, a caboose—were strewn about like someone had tossed down a handful of kindling wood. Steam locomotives too were deposited at crazy angles." He vividly remembered shaking with fear at such force.

"That there had been people in those cars when the water hit was a hard and terrible thought. And the dead were there. People of course, their limbs akimbo. Some of their faces showed terror, some looked peaceful, almost happy. Also dumb animals. Horses, dogs, cats, even a few sheep, all were bruised and beaten by the debris in the floods as the poor things drowned."

Mik again put his hand on Steu's shoulder. "No one should have to experience seeing that. Or to die such a way."

Steu didn't acknowledge. "Smoke hurt my lungs and clouded my vision. Here and there, fires hungrily consumed people's businesses, homes and lives. Crowds milled, gaping, some rooting through ruins. Others, shrieking, were looking for friends and family in the crowd. Most were subdued, unable or unwilling to take it in. And the smell. It was just damp muddy wet at first. Soon the stench of death rose, got into your clothes, your hair, your nose, your soul…."

Steu looked Mik then Cam in the eye. "Dante or Poe imagined such scenes. This one was all too real."

He sat back, suddenly relaxed, almost weak. Rubbing his eyes, he felt for a glass of water.

Having polished off his steak and peppers, Cam took a roll and sopped the juice. He stuffed the entire gooey mass into his mouth before talking. Mik always wondered why he waited to talk until he filled his mouth. "I don't know this Dontay fellow, but if he is like Poe, I get the picture. It must have been awful."

Steu nodded absently. "Yup." His face brightened. "If you had asked me then if anything good would result, I would have lashed out, tried to hit you, I swear to God I would have. But, sure enough, over time.... Good has come of the suffering and destruction. Pueblo is rebuilt and has recovered, and now we have the tunnel. It was built because of that monsoon's worth of rain that fell in three days and its mud filled wave."

ACROSS TOWN, A MAN AND A WOMAN TALKED ON BUSINESS. The tunnel opening was a watershed for them like most other Coloradans. Business and commerce moved on, looking ahead to new challenges and projects.

Joe Eggers was a self-made man. Inventing, reinventing, and re-envisioning himself, he had emerged from a dirt poor childhood and more than one business failure or life crisis. Out of each of them, he made sure that his existence became a little different and more successful. For Joe, life was much like the weather. Sometimes it was sunny and pleasant, sometimes gusty and cold. He knew that it was all in how you reacted and adapted. Some times in his life he had trouble finding a nickel or a friend. Other times, he was near top of the heap.

He thought back. Twenty or more years back he found himself in jail. It had happened before but that was another story. This particular time, the last time, he was accused of hitting women and taking money from people who trusted him. That was a rocky stretch. At the bottom, he fretfully wondered what on earth he could do next. He simply took small step at a time.

Now he was a respected lobbyist. Joe knew his way around the Capitol. He was familiar with every bar or watering hole used by Legislators and their crowd. He knew everyone who was anyone in Denver and the surrounding towns, ranches, farms, and mines. He was proud that he knew who to talk to or about to move his clients' agenda forward. It didn't matter who the client or what the agenda, Joe could move things their way.

The secret, Joe learned, was that he knew the who's and why's. Ask about any piece of legislation or proposed legislation. He knew and could talk on its prospects of passage. That included who was on the fence and who would vote for and against, and why. The 'why' was important, even critical. Knowing why meant he knew the hotspots of the Legislator, knew where to press to get the result he wanted. He loved mobilizing leverage to manipulate the situation.

His reputation as 'the get it done guy' was hard earned and he protected it carefully.

Twenty or twenty five years back, the picture was different. He had just gotten out of the hoosegow. He and the woman Ella, the one he hit, were in the same boat. Ella was still in jail when he got out. He had his hands full and lost track of her.

Shortly after that Joe started his turnaround. A good lawyer did wonders. He remembered the man telling the Sheriff and the Judge, "You cannot find my client's name or involvement in the scheme he is accused of. You have no grounds to accuse him of anything. The charges must be dropped." And they were. That reinforced a lesson for Joe, that is, never leave tracks. Let someone else take credit, as long as you pull the strings and get the money.

Back then, he immediately started to work; it took patience, time and effort to rebuild. First thing he did was find a way to advertise himself as a lawyer. Technically he became one. No one ever seriously looked at his credentials. Only he knew his law degree was bought from an obscure upstate New York 'university.' He suspected but never took the trouble to learn if their post office box was their only facility.

Being a lawyer worked out well for him. Now he was happy and financially healthy. His reputation, well, he got the job done and don't ask too many questions. That suited him just fine.

Charity Hovus was a longtime associate of Joe's. 'Associate' was perhaps too bloodless a word. They were partners, conspirators, lovers, companions, friends, occasional competitors and once, antagonists. They had never legally married, but the world viewed them as such, and by now, so did they.

Back when Joe was falling into his rock bottom, she left town thinking she had a fortune. The two of them had amassed money from many folks. She was sure it was in the case she carried onto a southbound train.

At the time, she didn't know it, but Joe was in a fistfight and was just about to be jailed. This was going on just as she boarded the train. On the ride she learned a cold truth. Her case contained not a fortune, rather merely a modest sum. She got back on a northbound, unsure of the reception she could expect from Joe. She shouldn't have worried. Once she got him out of the klink they talked. Joe told her that he would have done the same thing if given the chance. He welcomed her back and together the two of them rebuilt their lives.

Past was past. They trusted each other, and business went on as usual. Now, years later, they too were focused on the tunnel opening. They wondered, what did it mean for them?

"Joe, after all the hoohah about the opening of the Moffat Tunnel, I thought back about how it came to be. Remember all the studies to build railroad tunnels in Colorado? There were a bunch of them over the years. Some came to a vote, others never got past the talking stage. At the time I wasn't sure there was much to them. I had tons of eastern investors who were looking for a home for their money. Somehow we never got around to boring any of those tunnels. Actually, the idea of a tunnel through the mountains seemed pretty far-fetched."

Charity got up and walked around nervously. She liked to think out loud and pacing the room helped mold her thoughts. When he first saw this, Joe found it a little unnerving. Now he was used to it. He understood that she wasn't really conversing or expecting back and forth. She was laying out and examining different ideas and approaches to the issue at hand. He kind of half nodded as she started in again.

"Finally the flood came. That was an awful trial for that town, Pueblo. All the destruction and death! The people down there struggled so. The hole they found themselves in was so deep they just couldn't get themselves put back together. Isn't it odd how a crisis or problem gets handled differently by different people? Some roll up their sleeves and do their best. Some cower in the corner and never do recover. I wonder why that is?"

She stopped, looking out at the early dark afternoon. "I wonder if it will snow...." After a moment she started pacing again. "Then the state inserted itself. Your governor called a special session of the Legislature. The laws they passed helped most everyone. They saw to it that the tunnel got underway. And more importantly for the people of the

Arkansas Valley, they funded the flood control levees and all that got built around Pueblo."

She sat down and looked at Joe. From long experience he knew that her meandering was done and she expected a conversation now. She went on.

"All my work to groom the eastern dudes paid off. That eastern money snapped up all the bonds and other instruments I could sell them. And the work went on!"

"Sure, Chari. I remember those tunnel proposals and all the talk. There were commissions and panels and papers with analysis and maps and so on. Some folks were talking about studying costs and routes. Like you said, mostly it was talk and nothing more. The City and County of Denver tried to work a deal to pick up most of the cost in a joint venture with a company. The Courts tossed it, so nothing happened back then. Later it all came to pass, as I figured it would. That flood was a kick in the backside to a lot of powerful people here in Colorado. "

He stretched and yawned, and changed the subject. "This getting up early to read at the orphanage is tiring. I like doing it, but it isn't easy. Getting myself out of bed, dressed, fed, and through the door before seven used to be no big thing. Not so much these days!"

Joe learned to read on his own early. He liked to compare himself to Abe Lincoln, reading and writing with charcoal on a board in front of a fire. His efforts weren't that dramatic, but he really was pretty much self taught. As a young man he decided if he had the chance, he would give a leg up to kids interested in reading. As a boy he sure would have welcomed someone helping him.

In Denver he ran across a program to help youngsters in one of the orphanages do just that. The effort was struggling when he started. Soon his welcoming energy had kids flocking to hear 'Mister Joe' read early in the morning. He loved helping kids, one at a time, to sound out words and build confidence around books.

Now he wouldn't miss those sessions on a bet. Three times a week, his morning hour was spent reading to kids and tutoring them as well. He remembered how learning to read had opened many worlds for him. It was important to him that others have that too.

He stretched again, thinking of the book he had read from early in the day. Then he returned to the story of how the main range tunnel came to be.

"I recall some kind of legislation for a tunnel at the Capitol. It came around and a bill was proposed maybe ten years ago. At the time we had been burying lots of people from the flu. The number of deaths had dropped way off and the epidemic seemed to have run its course. Must have been 1918 or 1919. Anyway, I recall a Bill running through the Legislature to study several tunnels."

He stopped to think.

"Now I have it. It was to study and maybe fund three tunnels. They were all over the state, balanced to get support in the House I suppose. One was under Cumbres Pass between Alamosa and Durango. That is a route off the main area. A train to nowhere someone said, and they were pretty much right."

Now she was half listening. It was history but he was enjoying the telling so she waited quietly, thinking of other things. Joe was listing the parts of some old piece of legislation which never saw the light of day. How he loved to pull out and chew over those things!

"Another tunnel was proposed for under Monarch Pass, between Salida and Gunnison. That was a nod to the D&RG

and its main route west. I'm not sure they really wanted a tunnel there. But the politics of the matter was, they had to be recognized." He grinned. "I love this stuff!"

He paused, savoring the interplay at the Capitol come law passing time. It was a mix of people, companies, greed, and legitimate self-interest. Those things stewed together, sometimes smoothly and sometimes not, to help define and generate laws and legislation. He yanked himself back to his topic.

"And the third one to be studied was to go under Rollins Pass, due west of Denver. That was in fact the keystone of the effort. As expected, the Bill to allow and fund these studies was blocked."

He glanced at Chari, hoping for a question or gesture of interest. No such luck, so he finished the thought.

"The old southern bloc killed it. Pueblo liked being the main city on Colorado's only viable rail line west. Wanted to protect the jobs and commerce which went with that. Can't blame them for looking after their interests. Anyway, they made sure that Denver didn't get their own line west. At the time, I half expected that something would come of the Bill. Of course, nothing did. The time just wasn't right. As we know, the tunnel did come to pass. Just not then."

Chari stirred. Not that this was boring, but it certainly wasn't captivating. "Sure, Joe I kind of remember now that you mention it. You had a great time working it, like a terrier gnawing a bone."

She smiled. "You sure do love that stuff! One thing I have learned, listening to recaps like this. One of the most important parts of the Legislative process is timing."

Joe was on a toot. "Yup, you got that right Chari my dear!" He cheerfully veered to a completely different subject. Chari was used to this, and took it in stride.

"Speaking of time, Chari, do you know how much time we save by owning an automobile? I can go where I want when I want, and the roads in and around town are pretty good. And I don't need to harness it up, comb it, feed it, let it rest, and so forth like you do horses. Or go wait somewhere and go with a hundred others, like on the train.

I drove the car to Boulder yesterday. It went well, and I didn't have any flats. Didn't have to stop once to make a tire change or tinker with the engine or any other adjustments. The road wasn't too rutted. In fact, it was graveled most of the way! Again, speaking of time, I got there almost as quick as if I had taken the train. On the return, I was able to start back and arrive sooner than anybody else. I easily beat the train."

Charity was always one to sense and grab an opportunity. "You're right, Joe. The automobile is handy and safe. They are making them easier to use all the time. The auto will take the place of trains someday."

"Don't be too sure of that, Chari. Trains are vital. The rail industry is large, powerful, job providing, and rich."

"Maybe so, but the car is so convenient. My money is on the automobile. People can come and go as they want. They don't have to wait on a train scheduled by some man somewhere else. It is freeing. You know, I wasn't sure I needed to learn to drive. You encouraged me, and I thank you for that. I am glad I went ahead and took the leap. Think about it, Congress passed a law to let women vote. If we are smart enough to vote, we are sure smart enough to sit at the steering wheel too. And now I love to go out driving!"

III

LOOKING BACK, THE MONTH OF JUNE 1921 WAS A WATERSHED. Steu's memories were not unique. Literally and figuratively, the events of that month shaped the rest of the decade in Colorado.

IN DENVER THE MORNING OF JUNE 3 PROMISED A FAIR DAY. Elsewhere the weather hadn't been so kind.

"Joe, look at this headline in the Rocky!" Chari held the paper up and read aloud, "Flood in Pueblo! 201 Bodies Found, Scores Lost, Pueblo Death Total 500 to 1500." She stared out the window, trying to imagine.

Most people would be fazed, overwhelmed by the misery and destruction. Not her. She shortly passed over empathetic thoughts. No imagining the terror of abrupt death, pummeled by debris in a wall of water. In moments, hyena like, Charity Hovus was ready to go at and tear into the leavings. She handed the paper to Joe, stood, and paced.

"There is money to be made there, Joe. Businesses to be bought for a song. Salvage to be collected, sorted and sold. Money to be loaned. Tools, clothes, food, building supplies will all be in demand. Whatever is needed, price will be no object." Being icily realistic, she planned how she would go about her business. "Right now they need help cleaning up and burying the dead. I will leave that to others. But when things have cleared up a bit I will go and clean up in another way."

Ruthlessness was nothing new from Charity. Joe knew that at some level, she cared for people and their problems and suffering. She was not the cold blooded thing she sounded like right now. He was not put off by such talk. He charitably decided this was just how she processed troubling news: looking for the silver lining of how to make money.

Tossing the paper down, he looked across the room, focusing on his thoughts. He didn't see the sunny lawn out the window. He too looked past the misery to the business and legal side. Looking at the big picture is how he thought of it.

"This opens all kinds of opportunities. They will need big money and lots of help to recover."

He too stood, paced, talked. "This will come before the Legislature, you just wait. This is big. I need to go see how bad it is there in Pueblo. And I'll watch developments. I expect they will need help. There will be something the Legislature can do to help them rebuild. That means there are deals to be worked. It will take work with and by lots of different people to get it done."

Joe veered. While he was on the topic of the Legislature he recalled seeing someone there. He snapped his fingers, wanting to share with her.

"You'll never guess who I saw down at the Capitol yesterday."

Charity shrugged. He regularly saw lots of folks from all over.

"No idea, Joe. Who did you see?"

"Dale Smertz and Ella Queue. I think. I had heard but wasn't sure if they were back here in Denver."

"Those two? Here in Colorado? Really!?"

She sat. "Why do you think it was them?"

"There was a couple across the rotunda room. You know, the round room below the dome. It is big and noisy, always crowded. Anyway, I was talking with the Speaker of the House. Discussing a couple of bills working through committee. Some will come to the Floor, some will be killed. Then I noticed …."

Chari, impatient. "And?"

He was thinking of something the Speaker said, and made a mental note to follow it up.

"And, a tall gangly man crossed the room behind him. This guy was very well dressed and self assured, not like the Dale we knew. But it looked like him, or I should say, a better groomed twin. Can you imagine two of him? Anyway, whoever it was, the guy is connected."

"The Dale we knew was disconnected on so many levels."

In her mind's eye, Chari saw a man dressed from the rag pile, smart as a whip but oblivious to social norms. "He could talk astronomy or business or naval strategy or railroad building. One on one he could make a case for whatever he wanted. But put him in a room of people and he was totally ineffective."

"Well, this guy was well dressed and worked the crowd as he went. You could tell he was somebody. You know how the crowd parts for someone people want to talk to or be seen with? That was him yesterday."

Joe looked squarely at Chari. "And Ella. With him was a well dressed woman. Up to the minute stylish. She wore a nice outfit with gloves and a hat, fine as can be. I'm pretty sure it was her. In a dress!"

Joe remembered her as a woman going around the country spying on railroads and stirring up labor trouble. And she wore only men's canvas trousers and baggy wool shirts, never dresses.

"This woman, Ella or her look-alike, also talked to people as she went. She seemed to be respected and liked. One person actually hugged her! Now, I couldn't really focus since the Speaker was deep into policy, looking me in the eye as he talked. I think he's ready to deal on something I've been trying to get done for quite a while. Still, I'm pretty sure it is them, Chari. Dale and Ella."

"They have nerve. I can't believe they have showed up here in Denver. And now you tell me they are parading around the State Capitol like they own it." As she said this, it occurred to each of them that people could say the same about her and Joe. Both buried that idea.

"I don't think they just showed up. I had heard he was back in town. They are a couple so it makes sense she is here too. I wonder where they went. Anyway, I think they have been here and we simply haven't run across them. From the way many in the crowd acted, they are not newcomers. My guess is they have been here quite a while, and know lots of folks."

Chari rolled her eyes, trying to digest this.

"The plot gets crazier, Chari. Get this: Ella was walking alongside and seemed to be guiding or accompanying the head of the orphanage I read at. Next time I'm there I'll see what I can find out from her."

"Find out all you want, Joe. Just remember that I don't particularly want to talk to them. They have always been trouble. You and I, Joe, are doing just fine. I mean, you are a well known lobbyist. And I am established as a securities broker. We don't need them. And we don't need the trouble that seems to accompany them wherever they go. Let's keep our distance."

A thought burst into Chari's mind. "If they're so well known and established, where did they get their money? Last we saw either of them they were running and broke. More broke than we were."

"Question number one. I agree. Then again, no reason for them not to be doing well."

"Well, it doesn't really matter. Good for them."

West of town, in their country house overlooking Sloan Lake, Ella and Dale were trying to take in the stories of Pueblo's storm and deluge.

"Dale, my God, look at this headline!" She held the Rocky up and read the numbers aloud. Her reaction focused on her four footed friends.

"Oh the poor animals! It doesn't mention the animals. You know that hundreds, even thousands of animals were swept up, many killed. More have to be wandering, lost scared and hungry. Dale, I have to go help."

He looked at the newspaper. "They are going to need all the aid and support they can get."

Glancing at his partner, he was torn. He admired her passion to stand up for the dumb and helpless. But he could sense her about to go off doing something that was poorly prepared and not well thought through.

"Before you run off, let's think on this. There is no doubt plenty of work to be done. Let's come up with a plan. I'll tell you what, we need to round up food, blankets, furniture, every day things. If someone has lost everything but their life, they will welcome even a sack of flour and a frying pan. I'll see if we can put together a convoy to deliver whatever we can get. And meantime you can be talking to your animal friends to round up supplies for them."

She nodded silently, then smiled. "Alright, let's plan."

He went to the telephone, picked up the ear speaker and gave the handle a crank.

Ten or eleven days went by as they gathered supplies and worked out a way to deliver them. They intended to go themselves and see that their supplies were used well. A few days after that they made their way to Pueblo. The situation was nearly overpowering.

The Pueblo Deputy Sheriff looked tired, haggard. He hurriedly brought the two of them up to speed.

"The Elks Lodge has set up a soup kitchen. Their building wasn't damaged so they offer a place to sleep for those with nowhere to go. The situation is bad. We have about used up our local resources and what we can find nearby. We're running out of food, blankets, building supplies and are glad you brought some. Hell… uh, pardon my language, ma'am."

"That's alright, Sheriff. I have heard worse. You all are doing a magnificent job in tough circumstances."

She spoke too softly to be heard with all the commotion. She realized it only because he didn't even pause. "Talking about building supplies, we haven't yet cleared the rubble and debris to make room. We can't even use them well."

Belatedly he realized she had said something, and looked at her. "Sorry, I'm just so tired. What did you say?"

She repeated herself.

He acknowledged by a nod and went on. "And thank you two for the supplies you have brought. I just hope that the State and maybe even the Federal government will step in and help. We sure need it. Dammit,"—he glanced apologetically—and forged on "the whole Arkansas valley suffered. Damage and death even in La Junta and beyond, fifty or sixty miles downstream. It is just so hard...."

Ella was impatient to get started. "Thank you for the update. I will set up my tent and wade in. Is there anything special you want done?"

She looked across a scene of misery and chaos. Down the way she noticed a pig on the loose, rooting through a rubbish pile. She didn't want to know what it was feeding on.

The lawman spoke, cynically, almost hopelessly, realistically. "Only a blind or deaf person couldn't find something useful to do here. Just jump in. Stop me or any policeman if you have questions or need help."

Something caught his eye and he started. "Hey you, you in the green shirt, drop that! NOW! Stop, I have to talk to you!" With that he strode off. Dale shrugged, turning to look at Ella.

She was overwhelmed at the wretchedness. What had been a energetic city's business district was now anything but. First thing, she decided, was to talk with local ranchers. Maybe she could get them to take in wandering livestock. Ownership could be sorted out later. And she had to find a place to care for and shelter the wandering dogs. Before long they would be feeding on bodies. Already some horse carcasses showed signs of that. Maybe the dead livestock should be collected and used to keep the dogs alive? And this was just one small part of the problem.

"Oh Dale. "This is beyond belief. The misery, the want, the pain... And the smell is ghastly. The place reeks of rot, smoke and death." She stomped and it generated a kerplop of filthy, oily muck. "And mud is everywhere. It is awful."

He glanced down to see his cuffs splattered, and nodded ruefully. "We brought one wagon of supplies. I can see now that even three hundred wouldn't be enough. The chaos and destruction is mind numbing. We'll keep bringing in what we can. The Deputy is right, I have to say. This is so big, so widespread, that the government will need to send help."

Within days, Dale's prediction came true. The National Guard was mobilized. Soon uniformed soldiers, some with rifles were patrolling central Pueblo. They stopped the looting and robbery. Mess tents, water trailers, and building supplies were brought in. The Guard truly helped to organize and supply recovery efforts.

Ella was preoccupied with the animals but soon the people aspect was an even bigger problem.

"Dale, this is terrible. Many workers got washed out and lost everything. This especially hurts the poor, the people just getting by before the disaster. Business has all but stopped. Virtually nothing is happening. No work, no pay. People, especially those who need it most, who got the worst of the storm, can't find work. They have no way to feed themselves much less rebuild their homes and lives. What can they do? What can we do?"

"People need jobs, I agree. Well, at least one set of tracks has been reconnected from outside to central Pueblo. Now that a train or two can come into town, the steel mills can start to work again, and pay their men. That is a start." He looked south and east towards the giant stacks and buildings of the Colorado Fuel and Iron complex.

"Once that starts up, the businesses around the mill will be back in it. The parts suppliers, the mechanics, the barkeeps will soon have and spend some money. That will help. Right now, like you say, the people who usually pay workers, small and medium businesses, have no money themselves. We need to find other ways to get money flowing again."

Dale turned and looked over the central, destroyed area. "There is plenty that needs done. Here's how I, we, can help. I am working to get a contract to help the D&RG repair their tracks and station. If I get it, I will hire people, put them to work. Like I said, that will start the cycle. They will have to buy groceries which will put other people to work, and so on."

Ella was suspicious of the idea of a company doing good in any way. "You just be sure to pay your people. Don't keep all the profits." She had a hazy idea of how businesses ran. As far as she knew, the owner took all the money he could and did his best to short the workers. She had no idea of the complex shared effort and reward involved in running a successful business.

Dale was used to this. He just smiled. "If I get the contract—and I should—I have just the man to run things. And don't worry, E, he will be sure to pay every man who works. He was station agent here until late May. His plan was to return to Denver. In fact he had just wrapped things up when the flood hit. He had already sent his family north but got stranded by the flood. He has railroad experience, name of Steu Wentz."

He looked at Ella, waiting for her reaction.

"That name is familiar." He could practically hear her mind working, trying to recall. And he could tell when she hit the jackpot.

"Didn't he run security for Moffat? Back when his Denver Northwestern and Pacific line was just starting? When the grade was being cut across the foothills northwest of Denver and up to the main range? Yeah, that's who he is, isn't it?"

She smiled and he did too. "I bet he doesn't remember when he ran you and me off the grade on Eldorado Mountain years ago. He was downright mean, but at least he didn't hit or shove us. I remember his man had a shotgun, and the guy loved to fondle it. But he never shot at us. Long time ago. Lots of water under the bridge since then! That was before you… became an investor."

The glee in her voice was thick. "It is delicious that now you are hiring him."

"Yes, life has twists and turns. And in his defense, he does remember it. Says he was just doing his job, and I agree. Like he will do now if we get the go ahead for the yard job."

THE CONTRACT TO HELP REPAIR THE D&RG YARDS CAME through. Dale's railroad background was limited and out of date. He had done some work as a locating engineer back in the day. Steu, now Steu was a railroad man. Steel tracks were his career, first as security for the Moffat Road. He worked over into operations and spent years helping railroads move passengers and freight at a profit. The lessons learned over the years served him well. His latest job in Pueblo was to manage what was, in early June, 1921, one of the busiest rail yards in the west.

Steu stayed in Pueblo for the time being and came to work at Dale's company. They formed a productive, lucrative pair. Dale had money and access to more. He knew the basics of railroad work. Most of all he knew how to leverage his knowledge and influence. Day to day operations were overseen by Steu. It was not an easy or short job, but eventually all the rails which had washed out were relaid. The railyard at Pueblo once again was able to handle the westbound traffic from Colorado and points east.

The two working together did good work helping Pueblo to reassemble itself. Their reputation for honest work, on time and in budget was well earned.

Even so, there was much to be done. A lot of money went into the town, not just by Dale but others as well. Still the city lingered. The proud old gal that was Pueblo was hurting. She wasn't on her death bed but she certainly wasn't yet in the recovery ward. It was apparent that some kind of a kick start was needed. There were lots of ideas but none went anywhere, for lack of money and backing.

Even in Denver, people took notice of Pueblo's slow progress. The National Guard had helped for a while but they could not stay forever. Economic activity was still slow and many homes, businesses, and lives needed help to rebuild.

IV

Reconstruction work was never ending. The days shortened; autumn and then snows arrived. In Pueblo and in Denver, there was general agreement that the State needed to step in somehow. The Legislature was not in session but many Senators and Representatives stayed in touch, working on issues and problems. Joe haunted the Capitol, talking and arranging and making commitments.

One evening he and Charity discussed the ongoing problems.

"I've been talking with Legislators from Pueblo, Canon City, and the entire Arkansas Valley. Their areas were hurt badly as we all know. Even with the Army in there things are going slowly. They tell me they need more help. The question is, how to provide it."

"What kind of help, Joe? I have people who will lend money for recovery. Maybe I should talk with your lawmakers."

"Short term loans aren't really the answer, C. They need help rebuilding structures and buildings and railroad trestles and grades. But many are afraid a flood like this will happen again. They're right. Sooner or later it will. What is called for, is flood control. They need a way to keep the water in the river bed and out of the streets and railyards. They need levees."

"Levees? What is a levee? You don't mean, levy taxes, do you? Don't they have enough to worry about the way things are?"

"Not that kind of levy, not really. What they want is a system of levees. The word comes from the French, 'to raise.' A levees are really just a long dam. They need to be raised up or built on both sides of the river. If done right, a system of levees will keep the Arkansas River in its channel."

"Oh. So someone just puts piles of dirt along the river?"

Joe went on, not hearing or ignoring her question.

"Most times there is no reason to corral the river, keep it in banks. It stays there naturally. But the need arises if—or really when—there is another gully washer of a storm. It really is too bad there weren't levees eighteen or twenty feet high running along both banks through town last summer. If there were, Pueblo would have had no flood. It would have been just a high water day, with the edge of the river up against the levees. Just big water running down the river channel. No destruction, no drowning, no fires, just a day to have a picnic atop the levee and watch."

"Why don't they just build these levees themselves? How hard can it be?"

Joe shrugged. "It isn't as simple as just piling dirt along the river, Chari. It will be expensive and take time. The landowners along the river will need to sell the land or at least give permission for the contractors to build. You can't just waltz onto private land and install a permanent change to it."

He thought a moment. "The builders may have to put clay into or under the levees, kind of a water resistant core. The materials will have to be found, purchased, and hauled in. And there are trestles and roads and bridges near and over the river which will need to be accommodated. After the dirt is placed and shaped, the levees will need seeding and so forth so they don't wash away in the first shower. Even after they're built they'll need maintaining, you know, repair and regrading."

She nodded. "So it will be a big complicated set of projects. Maybe I can sell some bonds, not railroad bonds, but…" Laughingly, she punned. "I can levy levee bonds!"

Joe groaned and rolled his eyes. She pretended to ignore the reaction and went on.

"Seriously, that would raise money. The city could build their levees or dams or whatever they want to call them. But how would the bondholders be paid—who will issue them and what kind of income stream will they generate to pay?"

One of Thomas Edison's new and improved lightbulbs went off in Joe's head.

"That's it, C! That's the answer! Bonds!" He grinned at her, then went on.

"We get the State involved. We call on the State of Colorado to issue. No, not issue, just guarantee them. That's better: Pueblo issues them but the State guarantees they'll be paid, principal and interest. The State stands behind the bonds to build the flood protection. Also, money from them could be used to rebuild the city. It could put the tracks back, restring telephone and telegraph wires, put buildings back on their foundations, and do other recovery work. And the taxpayers of Colorado, not just locals, pay for Pueblo's levees and rebuilding. That is a winner."

"Well and good, Joe. For the people living down there, it is really a winner. But if I live in Denver or Craig or Grand Junction, what do I get out of it? Why should I pay to build something that Pueblans should make and install to protect themselves?"

"Yes, that is the question. There has to be a way to do it." He stood, starting to pace again. "There has to be some arrangement that can be made. We'll have to give something that other parts of Colorado need or want. That'll take some thought. And I'll talk to friends in the Legislature."

She kiddingly gave instructions. "Well, when you figure it out, put me at the head of the line for rights to sell any bonds or notes or other investment. After all, I gave you the idea."

Joe was busy that fall. He worked with Legislators and Pueblo County officials and business owners. Over time, they discussed many ways to solve the Pueblo problem. No matter how they sliced it, it came down to government. It would turn out to be a classic governmental compromise: it took much time to negotiate, had lots of moving parts, offered something for most everyone, and it cost money. Snow was flying before it started to come together.

THE HEADLINE IN THE ROCKY MOUNTAIN NEWS SHOUTED, 'Governor calls Special Session.'

Joe knew the announcement was coming and was glad to see it finally made public. Pueblo and the Ark Valley were in trouble but most Coloradans had gone on with their lives. Very few knew or cared that Joe and others were at work. Behind the scenes ground had been prepared for a Special Session, a rare meeting of the Legislature.

The laws on the books made clear that a Special Session could be called to address just one problem. The named purpose of this one was to address the rebuilding needs of Pueblo, Canon City, and the affected lower Arkansas valley towns. Joe was confident that those areas would get relief, real help, out of the Session.

Part of Joe's work in the negotiations was to be familiar with the needs down there. He was home, just back from yet one more fact finding trip. The story was bleak.

"The place still stinks, Chari. It has been months, but it reeks. The funk of decay sits over what was a busy and lucrative downtown. At least now there is train service. The various lines are sharing some of the track into and out of town. That is a scheduling nightmare, one of many those folks suffer. And serious cleanup has been undertaken. At least now the dead animals have been taken away and buried. The cleanup has a grim side. Sad to say, bodies—people—are still being found in the mud and ruins. I mean both in town and downstream. At least survivors, some of them, are finding out where their loved ones died."

At this he made the sign of the cross, which flabbergasted Chari. She had never seen him do that, didn't even know he knew how. He acted like he didn't see her surprise. Actually, he just ignored it and continued.

"The main street is cleared and open for traffic. There aren't many folks around but those that are, can now get around. But many of the businesses are pretty much gone. Empty lots or ruins stand along the sides. Only a few have started rebuilding."

'Why? If the streets are clear why don't the stores reopen?"

"You need to see it. Like I said, empty lots and ruins are the rule there. There are few undamaged buildings. Train capacity to bring in goods is limited. And if they could bring in tons, it would do no good. The main thing is people have little money. Even if there were goods to be had, none would get bought. Affairs are at a standstill."

"Oh." She tried to imagine such devastation. "So, the Governor's call for a Special Session is meant to help them?"

"Yup."

Joe was going into a meeting of lawmakers. He rehearsed the lines and anticipated questions. In his mind, he was speaking in front of the Legislators.

"I say you should enact a law that allows the State to form a taxing district. It also allows the State to sponsor, maybe guarantee, the sale of bonds. Taxes on members in the district will go to pay the bonds off. This solves the problem: It will bring in money up front to pay for improvements and recovery. The affected areas pay for the repairs over time. And it will be good for the local area. As the recovery takes effect tax income will climb and the bonds get paid off."

He expected opposition, likely from someone like the sheep rancher from Craig. The Representative for a district up in northwest Colorado spoke up. His constituents made livings from coal mining and ranching. He was a skeptical country boy, or at least that is what he wanted folks to believe. Joe knew his would be tough questions, like, 'All well and good, at least for Pueblo. Tell me again, why should the State guarantee the bonds? Why should my constituents be involved?'

Joe had the comeback to that down pat. 'It will improve the bonds' quality. That means they will be easier to sell on the markets. The higher the quality the more they will sell for, the quicker we get work going, and get them paid off.'"

Joe looked around the imaginary committee room. In his mind's eye, the proposal was well received.

Preparation was eighty percent of the battle, Joe thought to himself. He was satisfied with his lines. Another part of preparation: He was glad he had leaned on the Speaker of the House. The man had a lot of irons in the fire, but had agreed to persuade the Governor to call a Special Session to get it done.

Back to reality, he looked at Chari. "God knows Pueblo needs the help." This escaped his lips, kind of a mutter, and Chari didn't hear it.

He half nodded, then spoke with projection to be heard.

"Charity, it looks like we may be able to help Pueblo. I am going to the Statehouse to meet with some Reps and Senators."

"Remember me, Joe, if it comes to bonds. I have lawyer friends who can work to issue any bonds you—or the State—may choose to put out for sale. You and I can have a nice commission on all we handle. And there are hungry investors galore who will snap up State backed bonds."

She hesitated, then decided to throw out the idea she had been kicking around. "Maybe there will be a consulting fee in it for you or me?"

His expression, not quite a smile, was noncommittal. He tucked that idea away. It was a good one, he had to admit.

DALE ENTERED THE CAPITOL, LOOKING FORWARD TO THE Governor's speech about what the Session should accomplish. He stopped to admire the murals and the rotunda. Craning his neck, he didn't see Joe come up.

Joe knew that sooner or later he and Dale would cross paths. He felt fortunate that it happened on his turf. He was comfortable and confident in the Statehouse. Not sure of how Dale would act, he decided to be cordial. Bygones were just that, in the past, and he was happy for them to stay there.

He quietly approached, extending his hand.

"Dale Smertz! How are you, old friend? I have to say I'm surprised. I didn't really expect to see you again." He smiled. "I thought maybe you'd be scouting for a railroad up north or something like that."

Dale too figured it was just a matter of time before he and Joe met. Dale was a businessman and generally stayed away from politics. He had little use for 'lobbyists' and the government in general but felt he had to watch them. He had no complaints about his life and felt pretty much the same conclusion about Joe. The past was past and let it stay buried. That said, he certainly didn't consider Joe Eggers a friend. But he didn't want or need another enemy. He put on an easy grin, not a sneer nor was it warm and friendly.

"Hello Eggers. Haven't thought of you in years myself. How is Charity? Somehow I expected that you and she would be somewhere else yourselves. Pushing securities or investments down south or maybe in Cuba."

He chuckled, unamused, and stuck out his hand. "How are you, Joe? I hear you are the lobbyist." He emphasized 'the.' "Yup, people tell me that you are the man to see if you want to get things done here under the Capitol dome."

"You flatter me, Dale. I work as a consultant and lobbyist, yes. I can help folks who have something they need to get in front of the Legislature and Governor." He tried to look modest. He knew his reputation was strong and was proud of it.

"What brings you here today?" Both were aware he hadn't really denied Dale's description.

"Just following developments. My company has been doing some work to help unscramble downtown Pueblo. What a mess! So, I'm glad to see the Governor is getting off the fence. Pueblo and pretty much the entire Arkansas Valley got hit hard, and people there need help."

"Don't I know it." Without seeming to, Joe watched over Dale's shoulder as some Senators gathered. He watched them eye Joe the lobbyist talking earnestly with this gangly man few of them knew. Joe tried to figure if being seen in this conversation was good or bad for his image. How, he fleetingly wondered, could he use this encounter to his advantage?

Dale continued, "Like I say, I've been doing some work down in Pueblo. Well, not me, but my company. You may remember Steu Wentz? Ran security for the Moffat Road in the early years? He's a good railroad man. He is working for me to help with the recovery. Anyway, I usually steer clear of this place." Here he looked around the Capitol.

"But with being involved in the situation down there, I try to keep tabs on relevant Bills in the Legislature. I never used to care. It makes sense now, with what my company is doing."

Joe gazed appraisingly. "We need to talk. I know you and I have had differences, but….."

"What happened fifteen or twenty years ago is past. Ella and I have moved on and are doing alright. From the looks of things, you and Chari are looking forward rather than backwards, too. The future is more important than decades old actions. And disputes."

He held his hands up and smiled peaceably.

"Joe, I'm down here at the State Capitol for a reason. I want a shot at more of the work of helping Pueblo rebuild. My company has done good work and will continue to do so. And there may be more work to come out of whatever the Legislators decide. Maybe some new jobs entirely." He arched his eyebrows as he said this, asking silently for confirmation or denial.

The last comment intrigued Joe. Was Dale informed well enough to know that other projects were on the drawing boards along with the Pueblo work? He knew of the built in trade offs for the Pueblo bill. Just how much did Dale know, he wondered.

"I'll keep that in mind. Dale, we need to have lunch and talk. Must run now." He took a micro step back. "I'll be in touch."

"Sounds like a plan. Say hello to Charity." They shook hands.

Joe strode away. So Dale knew there would be contracts, and he wanted help, or a partner, it seemed. Or at least a friend in high places. Joe smiled to himself. He could arrange something along those lines for Dale, he was sure. It would cost him, one way or another. Joe was good at under the table arrangements. Dale wanted work; Joe could steer it his way. It was only fair that Joe get something in return. How did that saying go? 'Give a little and get a little.' Joe was an expert at that sort of transaction. He almost walked past the door he needed to go through. He veered towards it, eyes unseeing, lost in thought.

There was something about going into a Committee Room at the Capitol. It reeked of majesty and seriousness and getting the Peoples' Business done. Time to get into legislative mode, he reminded himself.

Coming out of the room was a junior Representative from northeast Colorado. He was from Peetz or some other one horse town out on the plains. The man had potential and Joe wanted to get cozy with him, legislatively speaking. He took the opportunity to strike up a conversation.

"Hello, Johnson, how are you?" Joe shook the man's hand, who was happy to talk to one of the senior lobbyists. Joe didn't wait for an answer.

"I saw that your farm bill got tabled. Not this year, huh? You and I need to work on getting that to the floor next session. I'm on the run now but let's have lunch and talk strategy."

He smiled and turned away, not expecting a response. He knew he just generated an entire off season's worth of gratitude from the freshman lawmaker. He went on into the room where today's action was.

Joe knew that help for Pueblo was on the way. The back and forth by senior leadership was done. The Bill needed voting on. Then it would be signed, sealed and enacted. The negotiating, the horse trading and give and take, was over and finished. The wording and provisions were finalized. He thought it a fairly good deal for all involved. His hand had helped guide it to the finish.

He fully intended to remind the powers that be that he had carried the Bill. No reminders today, but he would mention it now and again as he needed to. Also, he was sure he had several angles to bring Dale and his company into that loop.

Joe entered the conference room, looking to be sure it was vacant and ready. First he arranged the seating to his liking. He made sure to be sitting front and center. His intent was to run things since he knew more than most anyone about the Legislation. He got comfortable. Quietly he looked at papers, waiting for the room to fill with lawmakers before he spoke.

Every chair was occupied. Joe looked each lawmaker in the eye before speaking.

"I think we can deliver the votes for the State to issue bonds for flood protection and rebuilding." He went round the room, looking each Legislator in the eye. These were the lawmakers who counted for this effort. "It will be the Bill as presented by this caucus."

All of south and south central Colorado was represented in the room. Like most Legislators, they were mostly men. Actually this group included a woman, Mrs. Wilson. The good people of Park and Teller Counties elected her to look after their business at the Capitol. Everyone, men and woman, nodded or murmured agreement. They agreed on the need for a law which would help them and their constituents.

Whenever a problem or issue was tackled by writing law, there were compromises. Most in this group were not happy. But they understood and accepted about having to give something to get something. They knew how the process worked, that life on Capitol Hill was seldom straightforward. Even so, some wouldn't go quietly.

A comment from the floor wafted up. "Yes, alright, help is on the way. Well and good. Bonds, I have read. Bonds don't fall from the sky; you're talking cost. How about true cost of this 'rescue' package? What will be the cost for these bonds, besides repaying the money over time?"

The Senator from Pueblo, a senior lawmaker in the room scowlingly asked this. He had fought long and hard to keep Pueblo the only Colorado town with direct rail access to the west. It was actually one of the few in the region which could so boast. Today, he knew, that status was in jeopardy.

Joe too knew the tradeoff. He thought it the best deal attainable, and was content with it. He spoke forcefully and matter of factly.

"You know the cost. For help down south, we agree the State can also help finance a railroad tunnel under the main range. Note, we agree only that they can. Agreeing to authorize the State to issue railroad tunnel bonds is a small price to pay. The effort may never get off the ground. A tunnel west of Denver may never get built. Even if it does, it will take years, years! My God, man, Pueblo and the surrounding areas are still in tatters. They need help down there, now!"

The Pueblan stared. "I know that, believe me. My brother died in the flood. Part of our business washed away and most of what didn't wash out, burnt. I wish I didn't, but I know better than anyone in this building that we need help."

The tough old lawmaker almost teared up, to his shame. Looking up at the ceiling, he gathered himself. "Tell me again, what are the details of this tradeoff?"

Joe the lobbyist was not usually in a position to dictate terms. It felt good. He liked it. God help him, he actually liked it, even if he was trading in misery and manipulating people who had nowhere else to go. He especially liked it because until recently if anyone dictated terms, it was Pueblo talking to the rest of Colorado. He cleared his throat and laid it out.

"Well, the Governor called this Special Session to address Pueblo's problems. Express purpose of the Session is to find ways to help fund Pueblo's rebuilding. So, the Bill as written calls for the formation of the Pueblo Conservancy

District. It will allow bonds to be issued for flood control and recovery work. Such work to include building levees and new bridges, guaranteeing low interest loans for businesses, and general rebuilding. The bonds will be secured by the value of property in the district. Fund source will be a property tax paid by property owners. The district will be Pueblo, upstream towards Canon City, town towards La Junta. The tax will stay on the books and be collected until the bonds are paid off. That should be thirty or so years."

"And that is good for us. What else?"

"And our friends from Denver and northern Colorado added a provision." Joe knew the man didn't consider lawmakers from Denver friends, at least not today. But protocol demanded the phrase. He went on. "It calls for the formation of the Moffat Tunnel Improvement District. Bonds may be issued to finance building a railroad tunnel. Same terms, property tax secured by property in the district, to be collected and paid until the bonds are retired. District made up of the counties the rails run through. The aim is to build the long talked of tunnel under the mountain, cutting off the Rollins Pass Route."

Joe paused and looked around the room. "It is being called the Moffat Tunnel since David Moffat owned the railroad. Back in the day, he ran what he thought would be a temporary line over Rollins Pass. And he planned to take a few years to build a tunnel under it. But he ran out of money, and then he died. His tunnel didn't get built, but the idea to do it lived on."

The Senator looked at his colleagues. "And for years Pueblo has enjoyed the commerce and influence that came with Colorado's only rail connection west. No reason we can't continue to enjoy it. It will still be the only one in the state for years yet. And we will remain an important connection, tunnel or no. All the more reason to get ourselves picked up and dusted off, and build on what little momentum we have down there. We have a huge head start for rail traffic, even if Denver someday does get that tunnel through."

"Well said," agreed Joe. "And, don't forget. Even if the tunnel gets built, it will carry a line out to Craig. As it stands there is no connection to Salt Lake City or the western markets. So at best it will be a dead end road with a fancy expensive tunnel in the middle of it. Someday the road may be connected west but who knows when if ever."

The senior Senator rallied his troops. "Alright, let's vote for it. We southern Legislators would rather not see any tunnel built. And we have successfully fought it off for years. But that flood changed everything. We have to help the main city in our area. The flood happened last June and we are still in a mess down there. We need funding and we need it now."

The Senators and Representatives looked at each other, again nodding and murmuring agreement. They filed out, walking towards their respective Chambers, ready to vote as agreed.

Joe was confident of passage. He was tired, wrung out. Learning the final vote count could wait a day. He stood aside as the lawmakers filed out, and went home. What he wanted was to go home and talk to his favorite non-lawmaker about it all.

"Chari, the deal is done. Flood relief swapped for a tunnel. Special taxing districts to be set up in the two areas affected, Pueblo and the rail route. They will each float bonds. The money raised will be used to finance repair and flood control down south, and to build a tunnel up north. They were going in to vote as I left. No doubt Governor Shoup will sign the bill as soon as it lands on his desk."

"So bonds will be issued, you say? How will they be funded?"

"A special tax will be levied on district property owners"

"I will start talking these bonds up to my investors. Did you get us a consulting fee for the deal?"

"No, Chari I did not. Adding it to the Bill would have drawn attention. There will be money floating around aplenty, and we will get a consultants stipend."

"You can't tell me how much or when, can you?"

"Not yet. Oh, and I saw Dale, Dale Smertz. Anyway, he will be bidding on levee work, and maybe on tunnel work too. He and I agreed, more or less, on an ongoing fee from him for my services rendered." Dale had agreed to no such thing. Confidence high, Joe was sure he could get that done.

"Dale! You talked with that leech? Remember what happened last time you got involved with him and Ella? Things didn't turn out so well. We still don't know if he was incompetent or outwitted us, but either way, it wasn't good."

Chari was torn. She wanted to get going on her upcoming bond business. But she figured, the less they had to do with Dale and his friend Ella, the better. Joe wasn't so sure.

"Yes, we talked about that. Or around it, really. Neither of us wanted to dredge up ancient history and bad feelings. Like he said, that all took place years and years ago. Time to face forward. And I think that is a good thing to do."

"I think it is a mistake." She stood and started to pace, focusing on what interested her. "Anyway, can we—you and

I—expect to share in issuing these bonds? Or better yet, give me first right of refusal to sell the things. You can use your influence, can't you, to steer at least some of that our way?"

"Probably so. I'll see what I can do. In the meantime, like you say, you ought to contact your stable of buyers back east. Alert them. If we have buyers lined up before the bonds even come to market, get issued, we can command first place in line, and probably a premium of some sort. The instruments should be good investments, solid with a good return. And they will be long bonds. It will take decades to pay off the millions it will cost to build levees or bore a tunnel."

A smile touched her as she silently ran through a list of people to contact. They would eat this up! Still, she was uneasy. Doing any kind of business with Dale and Ella just didn't sit well. She swore she would watch them close. She could use them at least. And maybe she could find a way to put it to them. That made her feel better, and she decided to write her list out to be sure no one was missed.

AFTER LISTENING TO THE GOVERNOR AND SATISFYING HIMself of landing a contract, Dale went back to work. He wanted to talk with Steu. His man who had run the Pueblo jobs was done down there, and was back in Denver. Dale was confident there would be more work there. He figured there were others who could do the job.

Dale shook Steu's hand. "Good to see you back in town, Steu. Welcome! You did good work with limited resources down in Pueblo. A lot got done, and you are to be congratulated."

"Thanks. After the fires were put out, we got the railroad reconnected. So now Colorado's only town with a direct line west is back working, moving traffic. Maybe not as efficiently as before, but freight is moving. That will help the whole state and the region. The station works, takes in trains and all, but more repairs are needed. Most of the major problems have been patched up and function reasonably well. Still, there is room for improvement. The town is slowly coming back. Too slowly, many think. In fact, I'm sure some businesses will never reopen."

"You need to turn that back to the D&RG, Steu. The problems belong to them and other Pueblans. You stayed down there long enough. Your family is here in Denver and it is time for you to be here as well."

"Yes. I was willing to pitch in, but I did enough. I don't intend to return."

Dale cleared his throat.

"With the legislation the Governor just signed, we have new opportunities. Part of the bill opens the prospects for a main range railroad tunnel. It will take a few years to come together. That gives us time to plan and assemble a team. What do you know about tunnel construction?"

"A little. As you know, my background is I started in security and moved to operations. I've done very little in the building end. Construction of railroads and tunnels is a different beast than running them. The past months certainly taught me that. I prefer operations to any kind of construction." He smiled, thankful to be done with his stint of building and rebuilding, then went on.

"If you're looking for help in that area, I think I know just the man. He has tons of line and tunnel construction experience. He oversaw building through 'the tunnel district' on the Moffat Road. You know, the front of Eldorado Mountain? It has probably twenty tunnels in a fifteen mile stretch. Cam Braun is his name."

Steu had a serious, intent expression. "Are you serious Dale? Do you think you can get a piece of this proposed new tunnel?"

"Yes."

V

CHARITY HOVUS KNEW HOW TO SELL BONDS. THE MAN SITting across the desk was the prime prospect on her preferred customer list. The head of a consortium of investors, he commanded purchasing power most only dream of. If she could have only one customer on board, he was the one. She needed many and knew that if he thought a deal was sweet, others would follow.

Let the games begin, she thought. She knew he liked to intimidate, to grab control of the conversation. The tone of his question told Chari he thought her just a pretty face atop a nice set of curves. He glowered, asking. "And you say these bonds are secured how? What makes them a good investment?"

Her response was memorized but she voiced it almost casually. It let him know he was wrong to think her a light weight. She resisted the urge to smile cattily.

"The bonds are secured by the appraised value of real estate in Colorado Counties the improvements are made in. That means Pueblo County for the levees and flood control. Also Fremont County upstream and Otero County downstream. There may be some others, the extent of the flood prevention needs has yet to be fully assessed. The other district is similar. It is made up of the Counties from Denver to Craig that the tracks serving the tunnel run through. In all, property owners are obligated to pay a mill levy for interest and principal. The precise mill levy hasn't been decided yet; it will not be onerous but will be enough to pay the interest."

The customer didn't expect such a knowledgeable, detailed answer. The bonds were sound and well secured. He was pleased at the numbers and as a bonus he got to do business with an attractive woman. "I'll take as many as you can sell me. Thousand dollar denominations, correct?"

Inwardly Chari gave herself a 'high five.' Outwardly, she simply nodded, smiled cordially, and pulled out some forms. "Let me get the paperwork started for your signature...."

LATER, SHE REFLECTED ON THAT EASY SALE. "JOE, THIS BOND business is shooting fish in a barrel. It is almost too easy."

He was reviewing some papers and only half listening. "Glad it is going well. It is nice you can add to our steady income."

"Yes it is. Between my bond sales and your commission from Dale and others, we are doing alright."

The two of them were alone in their home. Joe was suddenly alert. Out of habit he looked over his shoulder at the mention of 'commission.' He was touchy about money matters and did his best to be discreet and keep them confidential. This applied to all commissions, fees, and payments, not just the one he had just negotiated with Dale. That wasn't a commission; it was a kickback. He was especially careful to keep it under wraps.

"Commission, Chari? What commission?" He smiled and gave her a meaningful glance.

Knowing she had his attention, she teased. "What commission my foot, Joseph. Would you rather I talk of your 'arrangement' or your 'consulting fees?'"

"Very funny. This is a private agreement. I know for a fact that others have similar understandings. Still, no point in advertising things." She nodded and he went on. "I'm glad your sales are going well. Make hay while the sun shines and all…."

Chari smiled, then frowned. "The sun shines often but it goes down every day. You and I need to be thinking about the future. These bonds, these big projects, won't last forever. We need to be on the lookout for other sources of income. Not immediately, but we need to keep our eyes open."

This was a subject they often returned to, and it annoyed him. "Gee, Chari, can't you enjoy that things are going well? You're moving bonds and I'm busy with my lobbying and my 'consulting' as you put it. Isn't that good enough? He smiled, trying to take the edge off. "If you're not satisfied with current income, do you have any ideas?

"Oh I'm satisfied with our situation now. It is just that can change quickly, as you know."

"Well, if you want to plan for something that may or may not happen years from now, go ahead and do some research. I have my hands full with the present."

Thoughtful, she nodded. "It is just that things are going well and you know they can't keep up like this. We need to be ready if or when our current income starts to fall. Some day these jobs will be done and you will be retired or sidetracked from lobbying. That's all. Just trying to anticipate, not criticize or anything. Don't get me wrong. I'm happy with our income and our life, Joe."

He nodded, mollified. "I understand, and am glad you are concerned, C."

She should have stopped there. Somehow she just couldn't let it go, though. "I know I've said this before."

Joe thought, here we go again, again.

She went on, of course not privy to his thoughts. "Speaking of income, no good can come of money you can't tell the world about. I'm worried about Dale and his payoffs. He'd turn on you in a heartbeat. Neither he nor Ella are to be trusted, you know that."

"Things are working well. And my income sources are no concern of yours."

"Don't you mean, so far things are working well? Keep an eye out, Joe. Maybe you feel comfortable, but I don't trust either of them." And I am going to keep after it until you agree, she added under her breath.

Chari had started the conversation in a jubilant mood. Bonds were moving fast, selling very well. Between Joe's insistence on keeping a slush fund and her misgivings about Ella and Dale, her outlook turned from happy to bleak. She decided that it was time to take matters into her own hands. Maybe stir things up with a visit. She would go out the next day after Joe went to the Capitol.

CHARITY RAPPED LOUDLY ON THE DOOR.

"Are you home, Ella? Is anybody there?"

"Oh, hi Charity." Ella wondered, what was bringing Chari around? The two women ran in very different circles. One loved high finance, big money, and fancy restaurants. The other liked a workingman's café, labor agitation—time on a picket line was great fun—and feeding stray animals. About all they had in common these days was an interest in the tunnel.

The views diverged there as well. One thought it an impressive and enlightened effort. The other saw a destructive, intrusive and dangerous industrial site.

Ella knew Chari's being at the door was not a coincidence. The woman just didn't have random meetings. She had an agenda for every room she entered, every person she talked with.

"Hello yourself, Charity. How are you and Joe doing? Come in, come in."

Ella held the door open, stepping back for the guest to enter. "What can I do for you?"

"Oh, nothing really. I found myself in your neighborhood thought I'd stop in." Her goofy expression disarmed Ella.

"Ah." She expected Chari to continue, to say what she had to say. For once the woman wore a genuine smile as she came in and helped herself to a seat.

"Would you like something to drink? Coffee? Water? I just brewed a pot…."

"No, thank you Ella, nothing for me."

"I will warm mine up if you don't mind." Ella took her cup back to the kitchen.

She returned; Chari was looking out the window. Ella

spoke her mind. "Say, I hear Dale and Joe are doing some business. Joe's doing some consulting work or some such? I'm not exactly sure what is changing hands. In any case, that surprised me. We've all known each other for years, but that I did not expect."

"Nor I." Chari was still gazing out the window, and she said this in a wistful, 'just us girls' manner. Nothing more, no explanation, not even a glance over.

It was not much of a response. Ella felt like she was pulling teeth to keep the conversation going. This woman had come to her, right? What was the deal?

"Chari, I hear you are selling bonds for the tunnel. How do you like it?"

"For both. I sell instruments issued by the Moffat Tunnel District and also the Pueblo Conservancy District. Both districts need the proceeds for the projects being undertaken within their borders."

"And I hear things are doing well for you." Far as she was concerned, dealing with bankers and money people was like trimming toenails: a disagreeable but necessary part of life. Ella knew her tone of voice was uncordial, even disapproving. She couldn't help it and didn't really didn't care.

Chari seemed to ignore the snark but her response proved otherwise.

"Yes, they are, thanks." Now she smiled and looked Ella in the eye, a challenge. "These bonds raise money for a good cause. They offer impeccable security for investors. There are buyers aplenty. Helping improve Coloradan's lives is something I am proud of. I have found a niche." She looked out the window again. "It really is nice to know that I am helping people."

'Helping people.' This phrase brought Ella up short. It grated like a rake pulled across a sidewalk, making shivers course up her spine. 'Helping people?' Since when did Charity Hovus think of or give a damn about anyone else? What colossal hypocrisy! It was all she could do not to burst out laughing. Charity, helping people? Right, and ostriches can deliver telegrams too.

Ella had many traits, some good and some odd. One quality she lacked was self-absorption. Her life was largely about helping those who couldn't help themselves. Not that she objected to making money or such, but it had better be at the expense of the rich people. Everyone else needed help, she believed.

Ella never shrank from chastising someone for animal mistreatment. More than once she had criticized someone giving her a ride and been forced to get off the wagon. That didn't stop her from calling out the next guy.

Also, she would go out of her way to spite a boss, or to make a problem for a business. It never occurred to her that if a business had a predicament, its workers shared and somehow paid for that problem. Still, her motivation and efforts were outward focused, not aimed at what Ella wanted or needed.

There was a lot she didn't like about today's life. The railroad tunnel being built became a focus for her. It seemed to concentrate, to epitomize, all that she disliked about the modern world. She really didn't approve that Dale was a major contractor and was making money off of it. She felt guilty eating groceries bought by money from his work.

Then there was the 'fee' Dale paid to Joe. She wasn't supposed to know about that, no one was. But she did know about this under the table deal. A quiet side deal was not necessarily bad, depending on who was getting it. But Joe? What could he possibly be doing to merit money? He was an oily fixer, for sale to the highest bidder. And then there was his partner, Chari. Ella viewed Chari as a money grubber supreme….

Her thoughts came back to the tunnel. Sure, Dale was making money, good money working on building it. And lots of others were cashing in, Chari and her fellow flimflammers especially. That was all bad enough. And that was only the money aspect of the project.

There was a price to be paid over and above mere money. The cost, the cost, the cost…. Not only the money spent, which was plenty. More to the point, men and animals had died, trees were cut down, streams polluted, all for a railroad route….

These thoughts ran through her head in a flash and Charity had no idea of their content or weight. What Chari said chafed, and the friction caused a spark. Ella felt the flame of fury and tried to tamp it down. She knew yelling wouldn't do any good. Realizing that she should at least try to be cordial, she responded. Chari still gazed out the window, oblivious.

"You know, Chari, I have to admit, I love the convenience of train travel. No doubt it makes life easier and better, at least for people. It really does help lots of folks like you say."

Chari was mystified by this platitude. "Yes, I guess it does."

"But sure is hard on animals."

"Yes, that may be so. A few trees get cut, and a few animals are chased away."

Chari couldn't believe she was hearing even mild criticism of the tunnel. Didn't this addled woman realize how much it would help Colorado and the region and her precious workers? How much money could be made by many people, working to improve their lives? Have a home? Eat good food?

For some crazy reason, probably triggered by 'good food' Chari's mind went off on a tangent. The vagaries of the English language flooded her mind. She considered the words precious and previous: one or two letter's difference in spelling with dramatic effect on pronunciation. Ratio and patio. Ration and passion. Garden and guardian. People in a steeple. Pressure and Cheshire: different spelling, similar pronunciation. How odd! Her thoughts floated in this strange word patch for what seemed some time, but was really only a second or two.

Wrenching her mind off wordplay, it came back to the tunnel and her part in it. She, Charity Hovus, was helping to make it happen! She was one hundred percent behind it. If she hadn't sold bonds like crazy the Moffat Tunnel Commission might never have gotten the project started. And Pueblo would drown yet again with the next big rain.

She looked blankly and quizzically at Ella, her expression flounder like. Here was miss smarty face do-gooder Ella. And she was talking about train travel being hard on animals. Animals! So what?

Ella took the flounder look not as vacant but hostile. The flame of anger that was tamped down suddenly blazed up. She lost it. Her voice came back, not soft and appeasing, but forceful and loud.

"But don't you see? Your fancy iron road cuts through the forest, with a wide swath. Everything is cleared out there. Everything, every bush and tree and clump of grass. That forest is where deer and moose and rabbits and chipmunks live. The tracks cuts their home in two! How would you like that, Chari? How would you like a huge swath cut through your posh living room?"

Chari was ready for this sort of reaction. Time to throw fuel on Ella's fire. She was, after all, content with, even proud of her role in financing the tunnel. And she was always happy to rile things up. So to start, she pretended to ignore the question.

Ella, again, even louder and talking fast.

"Chari. How would you like it if rails got put through your home, cutting it in half? And you had no say in it at all. With much of the area around it flattened and scraped down to the mud just to make way? And then listen to a big noisy machine clanking through at any hour? That is what we're doing to the elk and bears with this railroad."

"Bears? Elk? Who cares?!" Chari stared, wide eyed with pretend disbelief.

The knife was inserted to good effect. Now she twisted it.

"No one gives a damn about your elk! Get into the twentieth century, girl! This is the modern age. We work, we travel, we fly, we drive autos, we call on the telephone. We do not squat around admiring wild beasts or worry about their feelings!"

Surprised and angry, Ella almost backed down. The spark flared anew. Now she talked really fast.

"Charity Hovus, you, you... Judas! You are nothing but a cash grubber! You get your dainty hands and your very soul soiled by flogging those bonds. Bonds sold to rich men who fund dirty, evil work! Tell me, what is more important? Your bank balance or the lives of our fellow four legged Coloradans?"

She knew how Chari would answer that but it sure felt good to ask the question. "You seem to be more worried about selling some bogus railroad bonds than you are about the forest and the wild game trying to survive out there."

Pausing, her own eyes wide now, she added her worst fear. "This railroad of yours will bring new people, settlers, who will crowd them even more. Even more."

Ella was on a toot. "And how about all the horses your fancy railroad will put out of work? Will they be cared for or abandoned? Will they have a good life and be put to work and have a barn to stay in? Will there even be barns, with all the land being sold to settlers? Do you even care?"

Riling Ella was one thing, and Chari enjoyed it. Perhaps Ella was giving a little more than bargained for. By now, Chari didn't care. She was starting to see red herself.

"How dare you call these investments bogus? If not for me, this tunnel would be just another project, talked about but never done. Life wouldn't be getting better. And your Dale would still be a no account trouble maker. And you would be too. We'd all be walking or riding horse to get anywhere. You had better take that back!" She drew a hand back, as if to slap.

Ella was quite angry herself. She got into Chari's face, yelling, just daring her to take a swing.

"I will not. Bogus! Bogus! Bogus! Who cares about your stupid money? You will do almost anything to get it. I'll bet the men you know love to buy Tunnel bonds from you. Just how do you make the sale, Chari? How do you persuade them? What do you have to give these men, Chari? And just how much commission do you keep, anyway? Does Joe know how much?"

Chari ignored the implications, but her voice gargled with rage. "At least my money is up front and public knowledge.

I'm not paying"—here she made air quotes—"'consulting fees' like a contractor we both know."

Ella heard the words, the implied threat, and gave it right back. For some reason she got a flash about another aspect of the tunnel, one she found distasteful.

"And just who else is taking these under the table payments? What is he doing to earn them? What would the editor of the Rocky Mountain News make of such an exchange?"

"And speaking of filthy money. The financiers are talking about bringing in water from the upper Colorado, over the range to Denver. That is more bad news for the elk and bears and rivers you care so little about." Ella glared, anger burning even hotter.

"And you know how they plan to bring the water here? They want to use the pilot bore of that damn tunnel! But you don't care, do you? Have you ever even wondered what the decreased flow from the stolen water will do to the River? And how will all that water affect the Denver area? And how will workers, practically slave labor now, be affected?"

Chari got even closer to Ella's face, yelling. Ella tried to shove her away.

"Dammit, shutup! Ella, All you care about is so called helpless animals and workers. You think you are so smart. And you think working people are so stupid they can't even think for themselves! You want to take workers' union dues and tell them how much money they can make. And you say I am the money grubber?"

Now Chari shoved her antagonist, her partner in rage, and yelled. "You're the one always collecting money for your animal projects. At least the money I earn, yes I earn it, fair and square, at least the money I earn goes to help people. Me and the people we work with and the people we will make more money for. That money provides jobs and pays for kid's meals and goes for rent and other good, solid things. Not like you and your dumb, stupid animals!"

Ella stalked away before she lost all control, leaving Chari who then started to walk out.

As she watched Chari out the door, Ella realized there had been talk of 'consulting fees' and 'people we work with' and 'people we will make more money for. She wondered what that was about. What were Chari and Joe up to now? Was she missing something?

OUT IN THE HALL, CHARI SMIRKED. SURE, SHE GOT A LITTLE mad. But she had put Ella in her place. And she intended to get some of the money Dale was paying Joe, and more of Dale's money too. She didn't know how, but she would. And she would make Joe see the truth about those two too.

VI

THE 1920'S WERE AN EXCITING TIME. DYNAMIC AND INNOVATIVE, America was headlong embracing the future. Nationally, the news was of aviation stunts and records. Barnstormers flew their planes around the country, stopping at towns small and large. They would perform stunts, offer rides and even instruction. Many a pilot got his or her first taste of aviation by watching a barnstormer.

Internationally, there was financial and political turmoil in Germany. The protracted civil war in Russia made headlines. Back home, the Charleston dance fad and competitions it fostered were popular. The Eighteenth Amendment to the US Constitution was popularly called Prohibition. This was simply a well-intentioned but foredoomed attempt to make Americans give up liquor. Trying to enforce it gave many a law enforcer headaches. Many a bootlegger did well; smugglers also made lots of money. And under it all lay the good economy. Jobs and consumer goods were there to be had.

Coloradans were interested enough in these topics. People knew that they really didn't much affect day to day life.

The hot talk was of that bore being punched through granite fifty miles west of Denver. From the tunnel's start in 1923, it was the news. There were other projects but they fell into the shadows. Stories about levees around the town of Pueblo had no sizzle. That was frankly dull compared to boring a huge hole through a mountain.

Most every newspaper had some article about it every other day or so. The fits and starts of the various efforts and its construction milestones made for good copy. Stories of every-day life for the work crews were sure human interest items. There was no shortage of topics. The newspapers vied for up to the minute reports and interest stories.

JOE RUSTLED THE NEWSPAPER HE HELD, GLANCING AT THE front page. "I did my usual reading at the orphanage this morning, Charity. Not books this time, mostly articles from today's Rocky Mountain News." He glanced to be sure, and for emphasis, said, "The March 13, 1925 edition."

Looking back at her, he went on. "I prefer the Rocky because the Denver Post's stories are lurid, even scary, for youngsters." He glanced distastefully at a paper on the table. The Post's screaming headlines certainly drew one's attention.

"Even though those kids are orphans, they sop up the reading and learning. Most are really inquisitive about stories in the news. One asked me, 'Why are the Italians invading Somaliland? Where is Somaliland? How come the Greeks invaded Bulgaria? Why don't they stay home in Greece?' Good questions, no?"

He rustled the paper, looking at a piece on the tunnel. "After an article about the projects here in Colorado, another asked me, 'Why are some men digging a hole through a mountain, while other men are building dams along a river?.' She wondered why don't we take things as God gave them to us?"

"Good question. A darn shrewd one, Joe, for a kid off the street. Sometimes I wonder about those kinds of things too."

Chewing on a bite of toast, she sipped coffee and swallowed it all before going on. "I guess we are meant to leave things better than we find them. Why shouldn't we improve the future for today's kids and their kids?"

A lustful leer crept over her face. Joe loved that expression. It was much more fun to look at and took his attention from Italians and Bulgaria and other nonsense. She went on, the look giving life to her tone of voice.

"Not to mention the income from the bonds I sell. That income does a lot for our own future. I like the commission on those bonds. Maybe there are funding 'a hole in the mountain and dams on the river' but they make a nice addition to our bank. And now it gets better every month. Still, I'd like to find more ways to grow our money."

Not that again, thought Joe. She just can't stand prosperity. "I think we ought to enjoy it while we have it. Sure, keep an eye out, but what the heck, life is good now."

That said, a thought on the subject occurred to him so he tossed it out.

"Along those lines, new trends and all. I was talking with someone this morning, with another man who reads at the orphanage. He says the new railroad tunnel will really open up that part of the state, the northwest. Open and enrich it even more than the railroad over Rollins did. He was adamant about something I find ridiculous. He says, and get this, that there will be a tourism boom for wintertime over there! Can you believe that? Wintertime, with its short days, snow and cold?"

He almost shivered. "If I want to go anywhere in winter, it is someplace warm. Give me Havana!"

"Oh Joe, you and your thin blood. Sure, I can believe some people like winter activities." She glanced out the window, hoping to see snowflakes. She didn't mind winter, kind of liked it. Her mind drifted and she barely heard Joe talking more.

"This is what is behind his prediction, I think. I read somewhere about skiing. From Scandinavia, the old 'Norwegian snowshoes,' the boards you fasten to your feet so you can glide down the snow. I guess it is the coming thing, skiing. In Europe people will pay to strap those fancy boards on and slide down hills. I heard there is a ski hill and a ski jump up at the town of Steamboat Springs. So it is already spreading over here."

This morning, the flakes weren't flying at all. It was sunny and blue and she watched as Mount Evans emerged from the clouds over the range. Its mass loomed to the west. Still he prattled on.

"Hills, we have. And snow. That area on the west side, over near Fraser, gets lots of snow and would be ideal for those wanting to use their skis. When the trains start running through the tunnel, people could come from Denver. For the day, I mean. And from anywhere else for that matter. If they are coming to ski, they'll need places to stay and eat. And one day they might want a sleigh ride rather than go skiing. All those things mean jobs for people...."

She stopped him, struck that this might be an answer to her income concerns. "I think we should look into that. It may be an opportunity for us."

Joe nodded at that, glad she had a project to pursue. Maybe she wouldn't bring the subject up every other day.

"Good. We can't look too far down the road, C. Let me know." He put down the paper, walked over, and kissed her on the cheek. "Well, I'm going to the Capitol now. Committee hearings and all. See you later."

ACROSS TOWN, DALE SHUFFLED PAPERS ON HIS DESK, MUTTERING and commenting. Ella was in the room but was busy. She wasn't really part of the conversation, or the monologue. "Progress on the tunnel is slow, much slower than we planned. This will take longer and cost more than projected. Lots longer. This is turning out to be more complicated than we first thought."

Shaking his head, he continued.

"I read that the Chairman of the Board of Consulting Engineers of the Moffat Tunnel Commission made a prediction back in '23. Guy named D.W. Brunton. He said, 'There are no structural features evident which could interfere with construction' of the tunnel."

Dale stood up, irritated at slow progress and focused on Brunton. "Wrong! Hell, he never set foot there. Nor did he bother to send a crew to check conditions or geology or anything else. Took it all on faith and on his supposed superior knowledge. What really happened is he just let loose with that rosy prediction. At least he could have gone out and looked at the site before he opened his trap."

Unbelievable, he thought, his monologue going quiet. This tunnel had been talked about for years, even decades. You would have thought someone would have done a little homework on conditions at the site. But no. And now, we find that the chief engineer simply guessed at construction conditions. And that casual attitude had gone on up the line. The governing board of the Commission hadn't done much better.

No oversight of the engineering or finance, no oversight on much of anything, just get out there and start digging. Somewhere, we don't care, just start digging. The whole thing got started quickly and on the fly. Dale first thought it shoddy, but reconsidered. He decided the planning work wasn't really shoddy, but it certainly was not well thought out.

The monologue came to the surface and he started speaking again. This time he actually addressed his mate.

"Talking about costs, Ella. Did you know that the Directors of the Moffat Tunnel Commission assumed all costs of construction for the tunnel? All costs! Can you imagine, on a project this big?"

He sat down, warming up to talk on a favorite subject. "They didn't check the geology or the lay of the land. There was no attempt to share risk or make the contractor accountable. They just announced that they would open the checkbook. And now, they are going to put through a 'pilot bore,' eight feet or so tall, parallel to the main tunnel. They say the pilot bore going in first will allow for learning the conditions. And they can put access doors between the two so they can work on multiple faces at once. I guess it makes some sense, but it is also two tunnels instead of one."

He shrugged, soliloquy continuing.

"I guess all that is good for me as a contractor. I can pass along any old expense to them. I might have to hire some egghead consultant or something, and it won't cost me." He smiled at that idea.

"I tell you, Ella, if I were running the whole shebang I would fire that Moffat Tunnel Commission gang, every man on it. For them to just assume all liability, sight unseen, is crazy and irresponsible. It is good for them that they have bonding authority. They'll have to issue more bonds, plenty more bonds, to get this done. You watch, you just watch, they will end up papering the town with debt. The tunnel will cost twice their current estimates, maybe more. And work will go much slower than they thought, too. Mark my words!"

Ella was now half listening. Sometimes Dale got on a toot and she just couldn't follow it all. It came too fast and thick. This was one of those times. She took a stab at responding.

"Slow isn't all bad, Dale. At least it means more jobs, more men employed. Which means more money going to families and children, and animals. All in all, I'd say that is good. Better that than the owners get richer."

A quick thought about more expenses meant more bonds sold. That meant citizens further in debt to bondholders, plus Chari would make more money. The thought flashed through her head and disappeared. It scampered away, leaving a trace of unease. She wanted to track it down but couldn't.

Dale didn't respond so she turned the pages of the paper, scanning headlines.

"Look at this! The state of Tennessee has a law against teaching the theory of evolution, and some high school teacher flouted it. To his sorrow. His name is Scopes, John T. Scopes, and he taught the theory. It comes as no surprise that he has been charged with a crime. Trial date yet to be set." She chuckled. "Some really stupid laws get passed and enforced, don't they, Dale?"

Dale didn't hear at first. He was up to his neck in Moffat Tunnel matters, and was still put out with the actions of Mr. Brunton, the Moffat Tunnel Commission, and their wildly inaccurate predictions and un-business like actions.

It took a few seconds before Ella penetrated his fog. He responded. "Oh, yeah, I saw that article. That evolution law is one which had understandable intent but unintended results.

Besides, who cares if students hear many sides of a question? Isn't that what learning is about?" He drifted back to his tunnel musings.

Dale ate and dreamed the dig project. Even watching slush in the gutters gave him ideas to improve drainage at the work face. Or faces, to be precise. There were always a number of such sites under the granite, men drilling and digging and shoring. He was off and running again.

"Speaking of that, we are learning so many things about digging and making a tunnel safe. Many people thought the book was written. Nothing more to say, subject understood and closed. Well... maybe. A book was written. But I tell you, we are coming up with a new and improved second edition."

He was in full stride, literally as he paced the room. "We're filling this second edition with new techniques and equipment and attitudes and knowledge. The rock men of course have contributed from their day to day work. So have the engineers and surveyors, draftsmen and clerks, even the doctors and animal handlers. All have helped make things go smoother and safer and be more efficient. We have developed a large number of new machines and techniques. No choice, since we are seeing new and strange rock and mineral formations."

Ella kind of nodded. She didn't hear the mention of animal handlers. If so she would have jumped right in. But she wasn't thinking about teaching evolution or learning about digging through rotten rock. An article she saw reminded her of something and she was off on a new toot all her own. A change in subject like she made would have given many men a sore neck; not Dale. He was used to her veering all over the room.

"I learned to dance, Dale. The Charleston! You'll love it and we will have to practice." She stood and moved. "Up on your heels, down on your toes, is how you start. It is fun!"

This, Dale heard. In vain he shot a 'help me' look around the room. No one was there but Ella who sure wasn't going to rescue him. He tried for two things: not rolling his eyes, and not appearing to be unenthusiastic. "Yeah, Ella, that sounds good. When the tunnel slows down I'll be able to get away. We'll have time. Then you and I can go dancing."

CREWS UP AT THE TUNNEL DIDN'T THINK ABOUT DANCING OR fancy new knowledge. Like rock men everywhere, they were alert and wary. Every man there absorbed the lessons the mountain offered, every minute of their shift. If you asked them about 'knowledge' they would have scoffed, but each one took in as much as he could. They cherished every inch of progress and loved every day they bested that bitch of a mountain.

The crews just kept digging, paying little attention to issues like engineer reports, assumption of financial risk or legal liability. They spent their days where machines worked clankily and dynamite went off. And they liked it that way. If you had told them they were some kind of celebrities they would have snorted in disbelief. Day and night the digging continued. The distance between the approaching work faces lessened, from the west end upstream of Fraser, and from the east, upstream of Rollinsville.

It was morning. A meeting at the west end was getting started in a largish shed. Location was about six miles south of Fraser. This group of men met at the start of their shift. Three such get togethers occurred each day, at the start of each eight hour shift. Always, the participants were men. Women working or even coming underground were considered bad luck. Such superstitions would carry forward for another fifty years.

As always the job foreman and the shift bosses covered the day's expected challenges. This particular morning the talk touched on Mr. Brunton's optimistic statement about the site's geology. The foreman led off.

"When we started two years ago, we knew we would encounter shattered, chaotic rock. We were told that we would dig through that zone in no time. We figured we'd be into solid bedrock in a few hundred yards at most. I'm not sure anyone ran tests or drilled for core samples, but that was the official line back then."

Hearing 'official line' caused several of the shift bosses to roll their eyes.

"Yeah, we know boss. But here we are, are almost two and a half miles in, getting towards halfway. Over twelve thousand feet of digging behind us. Four thousand yards! And conditions have not improved much."

This shift boss looked around, seeing nods of agreement. "Not at all, in fact. The rock is still shattered and unpredictable. Every drillhole is, shall we say, interesting."

Another man spoke up. "Interesting hell. Reading baseball scores is interesting. Working this rock under these conditions is tough. It is almost like we have to learn the trade over again every time we drill and blast. We are never sure what will happen."

Looking at a map and graph, the foreman nodded. "I know, the rock has pretty much remained fractured. It still requires close spaced and stout shoring. We have had to bring in 12X12 Oregon fir posts, by the hundreds. It is a good thing we can bring them by rail over the Pass. If we had to do that by horse and wagon, cost and time would be twice what they already are."

He looked at his men, and shared a little frustration. "Progress is slow. I don't need to tell you. You're living it. Frankly I think we are doing a heck of a good job." He grinned. "Don't tell the men—they probably know—but this is for you only. The suits are always asking, how we are progressing, and why it is so slow? Why can't we move faster? Hell, on top of screwy rock, we've had some minor water intrusion. And sometimes the rock is weird, something entirely different for a stretch, not the usual shattered granite. But the muckety mucks don't want to hear that."

"Well, boss, at least you have good reason to be behind schedule." The shift boss grinned until he saw the foreman was not smiling. Actually he agreed, and grinned inwardly. Outwardly, he kept his stoic and sad face. He had said more than he intended just now, so he let a prickly silence build before the next issue.

"Well, in case your guys get bored with our rock conditions, here is something else to chew on. We should be coming up on what the geologists call the 'Ranch Creek Fault.' They tell us it runs through the mountain somewhere near our furthest east work face. It cuts, so they say, right across the path of the dig. Apparently this fault is a boundary of some sort where rock conditions change. Dramatically. So keep an eye out. Of course I want to know of any differences, no matter how small."

One of the shift men cleared his throat. "Boss, I think we have already hit this Ranch Crick thing. We had a change near the end of last shift and I meant to tell you." He smiled impishly. "I got called to a meeting and haven't had a chance yet."

The foreman lifted an eyebrow then laughed. He wiggled his fingers in a 'come on, give it to me' motion.

"Yeah Boss, the rock we hit late in the shift is now dry. Its not the usual mishmash of shattered granite and basalt. But get this: when exposed to the air, it flows! Not fast like water. It is really odd, thick and almost syrupy. But for the color, it is as if a hundred barrels of molasses got loose."

"Molasses? What the hell?"

"Yeah, boss, molasses. It is the strangest thing. I've seen a lot of stuff over thirty years down in the hard rock but this takes the cake. Or the pancake...." He smirked; coworkers groaned. He thought back on the muck slowly flowing towards him, and what his men did to stop it.

He looked around at his coworkers, happy to have the floor. "Oddly, you can easily block it, and then it is alright. You can stop it from flowing or oozing, nice as pecan pie." More groans. "Seriously. Last night we had no shoring or metal sheeting at hand. There was a stack of hay bales. We figured, what the hell, and threw up a dam with them. The flow stopped like it was fancy reinforced concrete, not hay! That won't work for long, of course, but at least it got things back under control. We'll have to do something to finish it off. Maybe encase that stretch with steel or concrete?"

"We'll probably have to do that. Just keep doing what you did and we'll get someone in to look at it."

"Okay, Boss. We need more hay bales."

The foreman nodded. "You'll have them."

He had a question and was pretty sure he knew the answer but asked anyway. "Any indication you have just a small or short stretch of this gumbo? I never thought I'd want to see more shattered rock but at least we know how to work with that."

"No, Boss, can't tell how long it is. Just looking, no end was in sight at end of shift. It is probably just too early to tell how long it will last. What's next? A flood or something?"

"Boss," another grinning shift boss asked, "Are they hitting snags like these on the east side?"

THAT WAS THE THOUSAND DOLLAR QUESTION. THE WEST SIDE shift boss knew his conditions but had no idea about the other side of the hill. There, men on the east side had good solid granite to work through. They had virtually no shattered rock or unstable roof conditions. They didn't have all the luck, though. They were having their own problems.

The east side job foreman didn't much care for this Cam Braun guy. He was told there would be a 'consulting engineer' roaming around his tunnel. And his straightforward instructions were to give Cam free rein. The man could go where he wished and any questions he had were to be answered. So, like it or not, he did just that.

Today, Cam was doing a 'walk around.' He hoofed it west along the pilot bore. The plan today was simply to look at the floor and walls, gauging progress. He made mental and occasional paper notes as he went. He looked back at the access port leading over to the main tunnel, and ahead to another. They were several hundred yards apart. It was dark but for the floodlights.

He was intent and blanked out all the noise. But there was something unusual. He looked up, stopped. What he saw was amazing and not a little frightening.

Water gushed out of the ceiling, a hundred gallons a minute at least. It ran down and away on the floor of the passageway. He exclaimed, practically yelling.

"What is this? I thought Niagara Falls was in New York!"

The foreman grimaced, smiled, then laughed. "Our own personal shower bath for the workers. It is kind of cold, and not the most convenient location for after shift cleanup."

Cam looked at him uncomprehendingly. The foreman responded before Cam could ask the question.

"Sorry, bad joke. It is flowing from a lake up near the divide."

"A lake? Seriously?"

"Yup. This downpour is from a lake some fourteen hundred feet above us. On Valentine's Day, a few months back, it started with no warning. Flow was at a rate ten times what you see. Of a sudden it just started pouring out of the ceiling. Thank God it was just water, no collapse or other rock fall."

"That could have been really bad…."

The foreman ignored the interruption. "And it didn't stop us digging. We were able to work around it. The water sloshed in and just flowed down and out."

He glanced back. The tunnel was designed to climb from east and west to a midpoint. Called the apex, it was just that, a high point. The apex elevation was fifty two feet higher than the east portal and one hundred forty two feet higher than the west portal. The pilot bore hadn't reached the apex yet. He and Cam were on the east side. The floor sloped gradually towards the opening and the sunrise side of the mountain.

Cam thought of a sketch of the pilot bore in his notebook, but didn't pull it out. He was still trying to get his mind around the lake.

"A lake you say? Are you sure? How do you know? How did you find out?"

"Well, like I said, the flow was tremendous at first. After a while the amount of water coming down dwindled but didn't stop. That seemed to mean a body of water not an underground artesian spring or something. And it didn't stop work." He was proud that his men had worked around this unexpected drenching, and mentioned it every time he could.

Cam found the repetition annoying, but said nothing. He simply nodded.

"Like I say, the water ran out and the roof was stable. No need to stop, it seemed. I needed to be sure, though. So I sent a crew out on showshoes and they climbed up the hill. There are several lakes up there along and below the divide. They found the one they figured was above us. Ice was thick on it but as they cut that away, they saw the water level had dropped, apparently quite recently and in a hurry. One of them put in a chemical marker, a colored dye. Soon we saw that color in the water flowing down here."

Cam smiled. "Tell me God doesn't have a sense of humor. He put a lake with a crack below it right over the path of our works. I'll bet he grinned as you guys first had to wade in water up to your belt loops!"

"Actually it was just deep enough to reach my knees. I can't swim so I kept one eye on the exit. You can imagine what was going through my head and some of the other men too!" He shrugged sheepishly. "Knee high was plenty deep enough, thank you."

Cam smiled. "So after a while, the flow lessened and you got on with boring your tunnel."

"We never really stopped, but we did slow down for a while I admit. Yes, the flow has slowed to a dribble. Well, maybe more than that, but compared to the start it isn't much. Anyway, we have dumped bags of manure into the lake above, hoping it will accumulate in the cracks and seal the hole up. Not sure if that helped or the flow lessened naturally. Maybe both."

"That is an old trick," nodded Cam. "Early day miners used a mixture of horse manure and sawdust to seal up the ditches they made to bring water for their sluices. It didn't make the ditches watertight but darn near so. It seems to have worked for you. That or the whole lake drained out. I guess there are many uses for horse manure on the job!"

The two men grinned, weakly. Cam continued. "You know, not to change the subject, but it is damn lucky that this occurred here on the east side."

The foreman was warming to him, and cracked another joke. "Why is that, o wise one?"

"Think about it, man." He looked around, at the work face and downhill towards the portal. It was two or more miles away so of course there was no daylight.

"Let's just hope we don't get a gusher after we're over the apex and digging downhill. If that happens, the water won't just be a nuisance as it runs out of the tunnel. It will flow down to the work face, and it will pool there. At the very least, work will be drowned out. Let's hope no men or animals get caught."

Thinking, Cam looked speculatively at the roof. "Do we have pumps ready for such a problem?"

He opened his notebook and made notes to round up some big pumps. No need right now. But once the men get over and start digging down hill, there could be. He certainly hoped they would never be needed. But if so they could pull water up and over the apex. But better to have them. He decided they should be car mounted so they could be wheeled in and put to work quickly.

"I'll leave you to your dig. Let me know if I can do anything." He shut the notebook. As he walked out he continued his inspection. It was a long two miles to the sunup side of the tunnel.

A YEAR LATER, EARLY 1926, LIFE WAS MUCH THE SAME. SNOW flew, Colorado sunshine bathed everyone, the just, the unjust, and those simply trying to get along. Days came and went. The levee and flood control work in and around Pueblo was close to being finished. That part of the big job was winding down. The tunnel, though, was not done. That wasn't close. The two tunnels digging from east and west hadn't yet met up.

Dale and Joe still had an 'arrangement' for 'consulting fees.' Chari sold bonds and more bonds. Ella continued her work for a safe workplace, womens' issues, and animal protection. Both women worried about the future. Ella focused on her life, Chari on her income. How would things look when the tunnel job was done?

One day Joe returned from a particularly lucrative and successful day at the Capitol.

"I tell you Chari, even the Governor got behind the Bill. In my wildest dreams I did not expect that!"

She barely acknowledged his cheerful news.

Whatever she was doing, it commanded her attention. Miffed, Joe looked her way.

"Chari, did you hear me? The Guv said he liked my Bill, and would sign it as soon as it got to his desk."

She didn't react, didn't hear. Spread before her was some instruction brochure. And there was a mess of poorly stacked papers. They looked like envelopes with several postage stamps attached.

After a moment of his staring, she came out of her trance, looked up and spoke.

"Hey, did you know you can buy an 'International Reply Coupon when you send mail overseas?"

Joe shrugged, still put off that she didn't congratulate him on his latest sweep getting a law enacted.

Either she ignored or didn't pick up his sarcastic, frosty response. "I don't send letters to foreigners. No, I did not know that. How would I, and why should I?"

He plopped down in his favorite chair, sighing at the comfort. He wondered if he should take his shoes off or if he would be going out again. Toe cramps made him forget the unlikely subject she had mentioned.

She forged ahead. "Might be this is a way to make us some money. A way that is out and apart from the stock market. With different investors."

"What are you talking about, Charity Hovus?"

She glanced at the brochure, as if cramming for an exam, then fixed him with a focused expression.

Sometimes, that expression meant she was on to something significant. The problem Joe had was, sometimes it meant she was on a toot and would be talking gibberish. Which would it be today?

"So, say you send a letter with an IRC to Mama in the old country."

"My Mama lived in Erie Pennsylvania, and is long gone. What is an IRC?"

"I know she is, Joe, and I miss her like I know you do. But please just listen."

She smiled. "IRC stands for International Reply Coupon."

"Oh." He eased up and gave a grin of his own. She quickly explained.

"If you do that, include an IRC with your letter I mean, then she can send a reply without having to buy a stamp. What an IRC does, is, it gives the other person a prepaid reply to you."

"Oh."

The dismissive one syllable response made her want to forge on harder. She had hoped he would be at least a little curious.

"I'm not sure if the postage is in the denomination of the sender's or the receiver's country. Anyway, you pay some amount when you buy the postage to send the letter from here. That way Mama over there can just write a letter and send it back. And, get this!"

Her eyes glowed. "She can do the same, buy an IRC over there!

"This topic is so darn spellbinding, Chari, that I have to ask, so what?"

He knew Charity was fascinated by anything involving money. And she was good at identifying and working angles to make more money. But for the life of him, he couldn't see where this was going.

"Think about it, Joe. Strip it all down, and what this means is you can buy postage in one country good in another, right?

"I guess so."

Getting into professor mode, she stood and paced. "Money does strange things when it crosses borders. What a dollar buys in say, Hungary, may be more than what that same dollar would buy here. Currency fluctuation, the eggheads call it. There must be some way to use that difference."

"Oh."

"Come on, Joe. It just interests me, is all. I'm just kind of talking through the idea and how the product is sold and how we might be able to use it. That's all."

She tossed the pamphlet down. For now she was done with it. Chari tried to look contrite and came out with a confession.

"Say, Ella and I got into an argument. Like many disagreements, it was a silly thing. I'm kind of sorry about it."

This was not true. She wasn't sorry because she had fun riling Ella. That cow was more worried about deer and dogs than about people. How quaint! And Chari had to admit, she especially enjoyed making money off of something Ella despised. Railroads and tunnels were for people, and she was happy to make money helping to build such things. On the other hand she knew Joe didn't want her to upset Ella. That might in turn upset Dale. He wanted to keep Dale happy since he was paying a good monthly income. But that didn't matter.

She was pretty sure she knew how to get around that.

VII

Building the tunnel was now in its third year. Working in and on the tunnel took up many peoples' time and attention. Three years of blasting and digging and planning and raising money.

For all this time, Dale's part in making the tunnel had been front and center for him. It was exciting and interesting. Every day brought new challenges and ideas. But lately he found himself trudging in a rut. More and more the fun was overtaken by the mundane. Hard to believe it was midsummer of 1926 already! Days hurried by. Like many busy people, he felt continually behind events. Reacting to circumstances was something he didn't really like. Seldom was he able to work his plan for a full day.

He needed to settle his nerves. Crawling into the bottle was out. From time to time he would tie one on but he didn't want that now. Daily decisions, fractured rock, unexpected expenses, it all kind of jumbled into a big gray mix. He sure needed a change of scene. His lover's love of dancing came to mind. That he even considered it showed how he was truly desperate for a change of scene.

"Hey E, is your old offer to teach me the 'Charleston' still open?"

Incredulous at this question out of the blue, she gaped. Dale? Dance? Voluntarily? What was up with this? Did he feel well?

"Sure, I'd love to! Matter of fact I know a club where they help people get the hang of it. Up on the heels, down on the toes! I can wear something new, one of my flapper dresses. Well, not new but you haven't seen any of them. It'll be fun! It is almost July so I won't need a coat. We can go tonight. Can't wait!"

Being a connoisseur of the female form, Dale had a low opinion of the new style, the flapper dress. It looked to him like a gunny sack with sleeves. It had no waist and covered the upper body, effectively hiding her curves. Maybe it was the chic thing to wear, but why was a mystery to him.

"That'd be nice, E. Sure, let's go tonight, after dinner."

"It's a date!"

She headed off. Looking in the closet to pick an outfit, she murmured "up on your heels down on your toes, up heels down toes up heels…."

The dancing turned out to be fun; they had a good time. Dale was glad he agreed to go. It was good to concentrate on something simple. He dutifully minded where to put his feet, preferably not on top of Ella's. Worries of the job fell away. It really was refreshing. Usually he felt like an elephant on the dance floor. Not this evening: Ella and the band members had made him comfortable.

THE NEXT MORNING FOUND HIM CHEERFUL AND REFRESHED. He actually looked forward to the day's challenges. Whatever the project would throw at him, he was ready. Good thing; the day would bring unwelcome news aplenty.

He gave his greeting as he walked in. "Good morning, Steu. How is business this last day of July, 1926?"

Steu looked grim. "Not so good Dale. Bad, in fact. Really bad. A cave in."

"Oh no." He asked dazedly, "Where? How bad? Were people hurt? How big? Tell me...."

"West side, yesterday evening. Bad."

Dale plopped into the chair next to Steu's desk. The grim account continued.

"Roof dropped. No warning. No one heard even a crackle or saw a waft of dust. There was just a silent drop. Of course the concussion was heard and felt. It got a timbering crew of six. We think there are no more casualties but don't know for sure."

"Timbering crew, huh? I know the rock on that side is fractured and jumbled and not solid. But we take steps to offset that. What happened?

"They were putting up the timbers, you know the 12"X12" shoring they have to put up every few feet over there. The poor buggers found a loose stretch no one knew about. A twenty five foot section of roof dropped, no signs, nothing, just wham. They had no chance. It just flattened 'em."

He looked up at the ceiling, collecting himself. "No recovery of bodies yet."

"Awful. Have the families been notified?"

"Not sure. The foremen have their hands full with the scene. I think the Sheriff is on that, at least I hope so."

"Find out. I do not want any wife or mother to read it in the papers or hear it in gossip. Make sure that doesn't happen, and keep me informed."

"Yes, I will."

"What's being done to stabilize the area?"

The phone rang; Steu picked up. For a minute or so he mostly listened, occasionally murmuring words and short phrases. As he hung up he stared at the phone, pale as if he had just met a mama bear and cubs.

"That was the shift foreman. Crews are working to shore the roof, clear the rockfall and retrieve the bodies. The whole area is a quiet zone. No unnecessary movement or talk. If gestures won't do, then they whisper. They're doing nothing but propping the roof up. Everyone is careful not to scrape tools. Last thing they want is to set off another drop."

Steu again glanced at the phone and shuddered. "He tells me they found the six men. Some still holding their tools. They had absolutely no chance, it happened so fast."

Dale nodded somberly. "I guess that is a fitting way for rock men to go. At least it was quick and they didn't suffer. But my God, that split second…." He silently wished their souls Godspeed. "So crews are in now, timbering the site? It will probably be a few days before work at the face can start again."

"At that face, yes. We want to be absolutely sure it is stable. But overall the work goes on. This is yet another time when the pilot bore being dug parallel to the main bore is paying off. We have run laterals between the pilot and the main every hundred yards or so. That lets crews work on multiple faces at once. So work continues at the faces near the middle."

"Small consolation. At least the job isn't stopped." He frowned, then smiled sadly. "Miserable thing to have to say, but I'm sure those six men would want us to push ahead. All of us left want to honor their memories."

Later, after the shock and cleanup, the mourning and the burials.

"These headlines are so sensational!"

Ella had her reasons not to read the papers. Coverage was usually shallow. Owners' opinions were barely hidden in the choice of news items. The editors who should be independent were merely tools of management. The slant of stories they printed made that clear. She seldom did more than glance and huff at the headlines. Today, it was with a frown that she shook the paper. Disgusted, she tossed it down. Today's approach and headlines were typical, she thought.

"Look at that, Dale. Six men die working in the tunnel." She dramatically held up her hands then flapped them down, mimicking the fall of the roof inside the mountain. "Six families suddenly without fathers and husbands. Six wives thrown on their own, their breadwinners gone. Many children who will never again get a goodnight hug from dad. And in all this misery, I bet that the company is sniveling. They're probably refusing to pay anything. And they caused it all! They hired the men to do hazardous work without adequate safety. No mention of that. All this 'news' story tells us is about the funeral flower arrangements. Disgusting."

"Ella." The curt two syllables took her mind off the venal editors and vile employers.

"Ella. Those men worked for me. I knew or knew of each of them. Those flower arrangements—and funeral costs—came out of my pocket. We are working with lawyers and their churches to see that no one loses their home. Don't you talk to me about what you call the 'sniveling' company will pay."

"Oh Dale. I didn't know."

"Over and above what we can do, there is the new law. The state Workmens' compensation program will see that those widows and orphans will be provided for."

She walked over and hugged him. "I apologize. I got carried away, and assumed things. I am truly sorry and forget that many people besides the six families are affected. It is all just so awful."

At first he was stiff, but softened to her embrace. "Apology accepted. And yes, it is awful."

"You're doing what you can. No one knows that. But still, can't the Denver Post give these families a little respect?"

Dale picked up the paper, dolefully re-reading the headline from early July, 1926. "Respect and restraint from a newspaper? Surely you jest. You may as well expect mercy from a mountain lion."

He looked up at Ella. "It is sad that those men are gone. We can't bring them back. The work has to go on. And it will. Those six were proud and able workers, and if that rock had stayed put, they'd be pushing on to finish the job. Too bad they didn't live to see it holed through.

She was happy to talk about something other than dead men and grieving families.

"Hold threw? That isn't good English. What, are they holding something that somebody tosses through a pipe or something? I can't imagine that—it doesn't make sense. What does it mean?"

"E, you slay me sometimes. Sorry, I guess I take for granted some of the slang and rock talk. 'Holed through' describes what happens when the two ends of the tunnel meet.

Somewhere under the mountain one crew or the other will drill a hole and rather than find solid rock, they'll hit air—the other tunnel coming towards them. They 'put a hole through' and start the final phase. In the pilot bore that event is getting close, and the main bore won't be far behind. When it happens there will be celebration and it will be a big day."

The light came on for her. "Oh. It's a rock man's term. I see. Yes, that will be a milestone alright."

He added, "And each crew wants the honor of drilling that hole. Bragging rights come with that, and everyone wants it for himself and his mates."

THE COLLAPSE AND ITS AFTERMATH OCCUPIED THE REPORTERS and the public. Descriptions of the workers varied with the newspaper you read. Were they workplace heroes giving themselves nobly for the greater good or laboring men sacrificed on the altar of profit? It depended on the reporter's writing and the editor's outlook. One radical rag even tried to blame the men themselves for the cave in, as trespassers in 'Mother Nature's bowels.' Whatever the description, interest in them would wane before long. That was the way of the world. Soon enough, attention would be focused on some other subject.

The six casualties receded into obscurity. But public awareness of the tunnel stayed high. Its progress and the goings on around it remained fodder for the newspapers. Work had been underway for years. The job took on a life all its own. New methods, processes and tools were developed to meet the unique challenges of the unusual rock and high altitude. There was innovation and invention aplenty. The public accepted and applauded the improved methods and technology. In this way, this spirit of invention and 'can do,' the tunnel project helped to define the future of Denver and northern Colorado.

VIII

IN AN EXPENSIVE SUITE ACROSS TOWN, CHARITY INTERRUPTED Joe's morning routine of reading the paper. "Joe, do you remember the tunnel cave in?"

"Yes. Sad stuff. That tunnel job is turning out bigger, more expensive, and more complicated than expected. Now men are giving their lives for it."

She nodded thoughtfully. Her grave expression turned lively.

"This makes me feel brassy and shallow."

"Chari, you're not that. What are you thinking?"

"Well, not to be crass, but.... I mean, I feel bad for the miners and their families and all. Some lives lost, others damaged forever. Terrible."

"But...?"

"But. Repairing this and preventing future cave ins will cost money. It will be an unexpected drain on funds. The more money the Moffat Tunnel District needs, the more bonds get floated. Bonds issued means more of them to sell, and more money we make."

The board game Monopoly would be invented more than a decade hence. She would be right at home with it. Today, from the tone of her voice, she may as well have been playing at that game. It didn't sound like she was dealing with real lives. There were no thoughts of a husband or son instantly buried under tons of rock, or the grievous lonely aftermath for the family. She smiled.

"So I guess there is a bright side to this." She put aside even thinking about being entombed under masses of rock.

Joe expected her to say something along these lines. He thought the world of Charity, but whenever money was involved, she became a profit seeking whirlwind, unfeeling and focused. Now he just accepted rather than judge, fight or discuss it.

"Yes, I guess so," he absently responded. The whole matter was sad and distressing. He retreated to the news of the day. Shaking the paper, he picked up where he left off.

"Charity, listen to this. Some Scotsman, name of Laird, has invented 'a new machine capable of wireless transmission of moving pictures.' He calls it 'television.'"

"So? Movies aren't new, even talkies."

"This isn't movies. Hey, speaking of movies. Did you hear about 'The White Desert'? It is a film shot up on Rollins Pass. It isn't one of the new talkies. It is an actual feature film, part adventure, part love story, with many scenes taken up there above timberline in the snow. It is being shown around to help raise money to build the tunnel."

"Yes, I heard there is an organ playing music as a backdrop, an organ right in the theater." She frowned. "I'd like to see it—see what the competition is up to."

"Sure, Chari. We'll do that. Anyway, this television is different from movies. The pictures aren't projected onto a big screen in a hall like they are. The images are sent and produced electronically, I guess. The images show on a small display in your home or office or wherever. Kind of like a picture frame with a movie in it. Some kind of a glass tube if you can imagine that!"

He thought a moment. "You know, C, this is the investment of the future. If you want a gold mine, a mother lode mine, we should get in on this."

"You may be right, Joe. But right now I can't worry about investing in some silly electronic gadget. The Moffat bonds are treating us well. Besides, I've given that IRC some thought. I'll tell you about it later."

Oh great, he thought. He wondered, what is an IRC again? With that rolling around his brain, he left and went off to the Capitol. He had people to see, Bills to promote or fight.

The day was reasonably successful. Some of the connections he wanted to make didn't materialize, but he did some good work nonetheless. That evening, Joe went back to his paper.

"Listen to this, Chari. The American Association of University Professors, the ivory tower crowd, doesn't like football. They can't be happy to simply teach their subjects. They apparently think we need their advice. The Association has issued a paper. It says college football 'promotes drinking, dishonesty, and neglect of academic work.' They want participation limited to one year for any one player."

He shook the paper indignantly. "Bunch of damn eggheads. They should stick to their philosophy or whatever it is they teach."

"You know, Joe, they may be right. University ought to be for learning. How can you concentrate on learning if you are practicing a sport or traveling to other universities all fall instead of going to class? How can you learn a profession if your free time is spent chasing a ball around and throwing other boys to the ground?"

"Maybe so." Joe tossed the paper down. "Who cares? In the big scheme of things, college football is not a big issue."

He snapped his fingers. "Speaking of a big issue, Chari, you called it. Like you said, the Moffat Tunnel Commission has had to issue yet another set of bonds. The ultimate cost of that tunnel will turn out to be over twenty million dollars, you watch and see."

"Good for us, no?" She grinned. "Too bad it won't last for another ten years."

Smiling thinly, he looked intensely at his partner.

"No, it won't do that. All good things must end as the saying goes. So, tell me, what is 'that IRC' you mentioned this morning? I wracked my brain just to remember what that stands for. And I still can't figure why you so interested in such an arcane, unheard of subject."

He stood and put an arm around her waist, hands wandering, and tried to walk her towards the back room. "Sometime you can tell me about these International Reply Coupons."

"Not now, Joe." She pushed his arm off and stepped away. "This is important. Don't make fun."

"Aw, C. I was just kidding. Talk to me."

"Well, we've been looking for a new investment vehicle, haven't we? At least I have, I really have. Now that the Moffat Tunnel and the Pueblo levees are about done and financed, right? Sure, there will be more bonds, some but not too many. The needs for financing will taper off fairly soon, and that well will dry up. We need something else."

Her expression said she was about to deliver wisdom of the ages.

"Well, this IRC is it." Then she clammed up.

He was quiet a moment, then broke up. He laughed and laughed. He almost had to sit down as he doubled over. It took a minute or two to catch his breath. How strange, he thought, and chortled again.

"Chari, what on earth? How can a few cents of postage compete with a five or seven point commission on a $10,000 bond? Plus Dale's ongoing consulting fee and others like it?"

She almost responded cynically. She thought, but didn't say, 'Ongoing? And just what does he expect you to do to keep earning it?' Holding her tongue about this took a moment. When she resumed, her tone was that of a preschool teacher explaining to a three year old that you don't hit.

"Bear with me, Joe. I have been thinking this through every which way."

He was getting irritated. "Spare me the lecture, Charity. I see this is important to you. Get on with it."

"Alright. I'll run it by you. I'm pretty sure it will work. I've looked and poked and prodded, but I can't find holes in it. If you see any, please, tell me."

Joe smothered another laugh, and he did a mock bow with an arm sweep.

"You have the floor. Please proceed."

A shy smile played her face, an emotion she rarely showed.

"The thing to do is buy low, sell high. Isn't that the thing to do? For any investment, right?"

"Makes sense to me."

"So, we buy these IRC's overseas, in Bulgaria or Italy or somewhere. Buy them in bulk. Bring them here and sell them."

"Why would someone buy them?"

"People will buy if we convert them from that country's postage to first class US Postage. They'll buy them from us in the form of US stamps."

"Why buy from us if folks can go down to the post office?"

"Well, that's the kicker. Who says we have to sell a five cent stamp for five cents? Say a stamp costs us two cents. Twenty cents for ten. We convert and then sell. Sell those ten stamps for forty five or forty eight cents. We double our money or more, and can still sell at a discount."

He nodded. "I follow that. But how does that fit with the buy low sell high?"

A conspiratorial grin played over her. "That's the sweet spot! If we can buy in a currency cheap in dollars, we come out ahead money-wise when we convert them."

"Oh. And how do we do that? It seems like a big if."

"Not really. We may have to change original currencies as the exchange rates moves. Bulgaria today, Japan tomorrow...."

"Sure sounds complicated. Plus, is it legal to undercut the Postal Service? Do we want to take them on? Or do we just beat them with service and convenience, or something?"

"Maybe its legal, maybe not. Those are questions and angles we need to think through."

They looked at each other, pondering. She broke the silence.

"So what we do is, offer a volume discount to the buyer. We hang our hat on something like that. Why should they care? Plus, we will be so small in comparison to the Postal Service they may never even hear of us."

Joe thought he got it but wanted to be sure. "Let me lay it out, see if I understand."

He assembled his thoughts. "First, we buy coupons somewhere cheap. We bring them home and convert them to US postage. Then sell them."

She nodded so he went on.

"And we work off of the difference in currencies between the lower Slobovian shekel or other local money, and US Dollars here."

She nodded again.

"I get that. But how do we make that work? We'd have to sell a whale of a lot of stamps to make a living."

She smiled. "Yes, that is a problem. But, if we do it right, we are in fact buying low and selling high. The spread will pay us. Pay us well. There has to be a way to ride this beast."

Joe wasn't laughing now. He wasn't sure where he got the idea, but it blurted itself. "Mexico."

"Mexico…? Oh, Mexican postage." She thought on it a moment. "Yes!" Jumping up, she continued. "Yeah, the currency is cheap in US dollars. Best of all, El Paso is just a day's train ride away. From there, the other post office is just over the Rio Grande."

"Maybe we should try it out. Buy fifty or one hundred dollars' worth of Mexican IRC's. Bring them back, see if it works. If we're right, that $100 will turn into something more. If it doesn't, well then we're not out much. And it will help us see the holes, problems, and opportunities…." He smiled goofily.

Now Chari laughed. She tried with little luck to smother a giggle.

"What is so funny about trying it out?"

"Nothing, nothing. It is a good idea. You questioned how to work it with such small amounts, right? The answer came to me, so simple I had to laugh."

"Well?"

The grin faded. "Say we can make a fifteen percent return. That should be easy. What we do is find investors to put up the money, and pay them eight or nine percent. They'll flock to us!"

Now grinning, she went on. "And we don't hawk the stamps. No need for us to go selling postage stamps like street vendors. We find somebody to do that. Pay them half a point and they'll be happy."

Immediately, Joe saw Dale's face. Bringing him in would be a way to balance the scales a bit. Take the monkey of obligation off his back.

She continued, not knowing what he was thinking. "You and I, Josephus Eggers, will work the investor end. People are making money today, and they want to put it somewhere where it can grow. Someplace outside the stock market and its ups and downs. The pool of people we can tap out there has to be huge, huge! Even small investors, people with $100. We won't need the heavy hitters."

Joe was seeing the possibilities. "And from what you say, we may be able to get and pay even more than your eight or nine points. If we can make it work for a twenty five or thirty percent spread, we can pay up to fifteen. No one else is offering a return like that. Especially based on a government document. That kind of payoff will attract people—and companies—like flies to a barnyard."

She twitched then paced in small circles. Joe at first wondered if a foot hurt, then realized she was just excited.

"I'll buy tickets to El Paso. For the two of us. No one else needs to know about this, at least not yet." Her face shone greedy, wild, even lustful. She went over, put her arm around his waist, and guided him to the sofa.

IX

Earlier that day Cam was not scheming with numbers nor snuggling with his wife. He was on the job, in the mountains. Time up there, even working, was refreshing and renewing. Today he was looking at progress on the east side of the tunnel. Crews at both ends were tirelessly digging. He wanted to see the headway being made. And be darn sure major problems were stopped before they started.

By now the job foreman was used to this visiting engineer's presence. He first thought Cam was just a management snoop, likely an incompetent one. But time showed that judgment premature and flawed. These days, the two of them got along pretty well. He looked up as Cam stepped in. The foreman had no fancy office outside the tunnel portal. A simple wooden structure did the job.

"How about that collapse? I feel for those poor devils working from the west end." Cam grimly shook his head. "A whole crew gone in an instant. Six good men, experienced workers all, who were simply doing their jobs."

The foreman bleakly nodded, saying nothing as Cam kept going.

"It can't be easy to shore up the bore with twenty foot or longer twelve by twelve braces. My God, those have to weigh hundreds of pounds each! Those men had to be strong and smart for that job. Sometimes that isn't enough. If you're in the wrong place…. Eight yards of roof simply fell in with no warning. Terrible. There sure have been lots of setbacks over there."

"Yes there have." The foreman felt a little guilty about that even though he knew it was like Cam said. Wrong place wrong time often meant bad stuff happened. He felt fortunate that his side of the works hadn't had such problems. At least not yet, he reminded himself. Somehow, and he felt bad about this, but also glad that if someone had die, it wasn't his men. That was wrong, he knew, but there it was. He shrugged it off, knowing it could well be him or his men under the rubble and in the headlines next.

"Yeah, they have had a snootful over there, but our east side has its problems too. Thank God, no fatalities, at least so far. That lake that drained on us back in February of '25 was bad enough. At least then, the water just ran down and out the bore."

Cam laughed. "The one you put dye into to be sure it was a lake, not a perpetual spring, right?"

"Yes. That was pretty darn easy for a tunneling mishap. It died away quick and we could pipe out the ongoing seepage easy enough. It seemed awful at the time, but looking back, we had it good. This last drenching was more serious."

There had been another water intrusion, this one more prolonged and costly.

Cam took a seat as he agreed with that assessment. "True. Like we talked then, being past the apex has made a real difference. We're digging down grade now. The drop is not steep, but it is headed down none the less."

A loud bang and crash made them both stop and listen. After a moment, with silence and no yelling, Cam glanced out the door and resumed.

"I guess that wasn't anything real important. Anyway, you're right. This last flood was a doozy. There must be something about the month, since it happened again in February. That's supposed to be the month of love, not the month of floods!"

There was more metal grinding and a few yelled words. The foreman stuck his head out the door then sat back down. "Just a load of muck shifting in a car, nothing to worry about."

Relieved, Cam continued. "Back to the February drown out of the works. It was just about one year after the lake that we—your guys—got another gush of water. Again it came out of the ceiling." He stopped, a goofy smile playing across his face. "That was stupid. Of course, it is the ceiling that things fall out of. No kidding, Sherlock Holmes!"

The foreman laughed at the corny joke.

Cam acknowledged, paused, and went on. "And this time around there was no lake to blame it on. Youall came across a big ornery underground spring. The flood of '26!"

"Yup," the foreman agreed. "And the overflow didn't run east out of the tunnel. It flowed west, down the grade, and pooled there at the face. Like you predicted would happen. It flooded the equipment but thank God the crews got out."

"That was a close run thing," Cam nodded. "It really gushed didn't it?

"Yes it did, at about three thousand gallons a minute. Three thousand! That is enough to fill a tanker car every sixty seconds. Hoowee, that was one frightening sight, I'll tell you. My grandchildren will hear about that."

Cam asked, "It ran for what, six days? I bet it spit out enough water to float a battleship."

"I've never seen the ocean, but I imagine so. That was something to remember. Anyway, after almost a week it slowed to 'only' one hundred fifty gallons a minute." He spread his arms wide. "Only! One hundred fifty—that is enough to fill three beer kegs every minute! One keg in twenty seconds! That is still one hell of a lot of water!"

He mimed the volume by spreading his arms wider. "By the time it slowed down, we were able to position some pumps near as we could, on railcars, and started to get the area pumped out. Good thing, Cam, that you saw that need back when the lake flowed in, the flood of '25! If we hadn't gotten some pumps and cars stationed nearby.... It would have taken us a week to respond."

Cam thought back. "Yup, that flood really slowed work from the east side. It was April by the time we got the water level at the face pumped down to a manageable amount. Time lost was well over a month! At that point, I thought we pretty much had the problem solved, or at least were ahead of the game."

"We all did. But no." The foreman grinned ruefully, as did Cam.

"The mountain gods must have been angry." Cam didn't really believe in 'mountain gods' but sometimes up in the high places it did seem as if someone was scheming against you. "Just as we got the water down at the face and could finally get in to assess the damage, we got hit with that big storm."

"I've been foreman here and other tunnel jobs in the west. I have to say, even for Colorado's Main Range, that was a massive, severe blizzard. Bigtime spring storm, it was.

The winds knocked down the power lines feeding the tunnel, meaning the pumps stopped. Of course that meant the lights went too so we had to cope with the dark."

He thought back to the confusion and tension of working underground with only headlamps for light, hearing the water splash.

He described the scenario. "No pumps and the water was still coming in fast. So, no surprise, the water level at the head of the tunnel started rising. Outside, the linesmen were working as fast as they could. Still, it took ten hours to find the breaks, fix the lines and restore power. By then the tunnel was full up to the apex again. But we got all the men out, no one hurt or lost."

He looked off, an expression of wonder and horror on his face. "My God, what a mess that all was!"

Cam glanced uneasily around. He suddenly remembered they were talking about events in a hole thousands of feet underground. Anything that could go wrong, might at any minute. He was glad that they were meeting and talking in a shed at the east end of the tunnel, not inside. He remarked on that.

"You know, I am impressed and proud of this tunnel, I really am. But I have to say, I prefer the open air. Give me a track hung on the side of a mountain any day over a hole deep underground."

"I hear you Cam. I don't mind this. Matter of fact, I kind of like the snugness down inside the bore. Anyway, that flood and the storm were something." He looked around, calm and easy like he was home in bed tucked under a quilt. Cam admired but didn't share the feeling. Even so, he was glad they had gone over and re-learned lessons from the disaster.

The foreman was intent on finishing the tale. "And then…. Insult to injury, remember? At long last, late spring, at last we got the place pumped and channeled the water out east. Things got dried out. Everybody was ready to get back to tunneling. We inspected all the machinery and gear. Oops, more bad news! We found a fine, thick layer of mineral deposit on everything. The water had some chemical or compound dissolved in it. And when it came in contact with metal, it left a deposit. Everywhere. Remember that? Machinery, rails, mucking cars, even hammers and wrenches. We still have crews trying to get that stuff off. Wiping, even with solvents, does nothing. It has to be chiseled off! We still have men chiseling on rails, drills, cars, you name it. And they'll be chiseling next fall when snow flies, I bet."

He smiled. "That bang you heard? At first I thought it was one of my men, hitting a pipe or machine with his hammer in frustration at the damned gritty mineral deposit he can't get off!"

Cam grinned. "Water damage up almost at timberline. What else can this mountain throw at us?"

X

Longtime friends, Mik Mas and Cam Braun had worked the railroad and played together for years. They knew the area, its history, its land and people. Like many others, each had long realized the need for a tunnel. In fact they were part of the original plan to thrust a tunnel under the mountain not long after the turn of the century. That never came to pass, primarily for lack of money.

They avidly followed the modern tunnel's progress. One of them was consulting in its construction. This day they were discussing the cave-in and its aftermath. It had been months but the memories stood out.

Mik remembered one of the last funerals. "Well, it was a solemn and fitting celebration of life, at least the songs and memorial. The sermon, I could have done without. Hellfire and brimstone doesn't need to be thrown in our faces while mourning a good man. He was the last of the six to be laid to rest."

"Yes, I agree, Mik. It wasn't the time to drag us across coals of guilt and doubt. The preacher should have stuck to the Ninety Second Psalm."

Mik was done with the memorial service. He changed the subject, looking back at the killing scene and the rest of the job.

"I guess the collapsed area has been cleaned up and shored to safety. I hope that is the last of such accidents." He paused, thinking. "Sure is odd, isn't it? How work from the one end, the west, has had rock and rockfall problems but has stayed dry. On the other hand, crews working from the east have had stable rock, but they seem to get drenched every so often. The mountain is fighting us hard, isn't she? She keeps throwing out curve balls and making us work extra hard."

"For sure. We can never become complacent. Just when we think we understand the job, there is some new wrinkle or problem and the occasional crisis. Rock work and tunneling have been practiced and developed for thousands of years. You'd think it would be wholly understood. Not so much…. This job, this project, has put paid to that idea. We have added whole chapters to the book on tunneling. We've come up with new ideas and new things every time we need to."

Cam drank his coffee, enjoying the hot bitterness. He loved talking machinery, and Mik knew he was going to hear about some new assembly of metal pieces powered and used by smart people. Cam was on a roll.

"Take one of our engineers, George Lewis. Longtime rock man, really knows his stuff. He has written one of those chapters himself. He watched crews, particularly west end crews, battle the fragmented rock. Most tunnels go through solid rock, not big underground piles of sharp slabs of the stuff piled pell mell, ready to fall at a sneeze." He stopped himself. "Old Lewis had trouble sleeping because he was trying to think of ways to make life easier and safer for those crews."

"Lots of foremen do the same thing. No one wants to see folks get hurt."

"True. Occasionally the nightmares visit me. Not so much about the tunnel, but about working the road over the Hill. It has been at least twenty years since then. And I long ago stopped day to day contact with running and managing trains. Still, sometimes my night is filled with derailments and wrecks and stranded passengers and snow and wind."

Awful scenes and memories mixed with stunning natural beauty crowded in on Cam. He pushed back. "Sorry, not sure where that came from. I guess my mention of Lewis dreaming about how to improve the tunnel work jumped me back." He shrugged.

"Anyway.... Like I said, Lewis saw that something was needed. He needed some way to move the work face forward, keep the roof shored, and move the muck out. He was sure there was some way to do that while also being easy and safe to operate. Not a simple task when you add in falling rock, lots of moving machinery, noise, and men using explosives. A tall order, but he came through."

Another gulp. By now people knew Cam, by sight and by how he noisily drank his coffee. Some found it offensive; some found it funny; most folks got used to it. It was just Cam. He set the cup down and continued his tribute to the engineer.

"To solve those problems, Lewis had a vision, or a whole idea, one night. I guess it just came to him, entire and ready. The idea was for a moving platform. It is a big gizmo. It protects the workers, allows shoring or plastering to stabilize the cut, and gives room for moving the muck away quickly and efficiently. And it can be moved forward as needed."

He paused, thinking almost affectionately of the giant steel spiders which remained attached to the work face even as the tunnel lengthened.

"I guess the formal name on the patent papers and so on is 'The Lewis Traveling Cantilever Girder.' No one calls it that. It is just 'the Lewis Bar.' It lurches along, spearing the face and hauling timbers and crawling with workers. Power for the work and its movement is compressed air and electricity."

Mik had heard of the Lewis Bar. "You know, that reminds me of the old Roberts Track Layer. You know, the steam powered rig that laid rails faster and truer than any crew of Irishmen. The Lewis does its work underground carving a tunnel, but they both improve and speed the job."

The Roberts Track Laying system was used in 1904 and later to lay much of the rail up and over Rollins Pass and beyond. Powered by a coal burning steam boiler, it couldn't sneak up on anything for the noise and smoke. It too moved in lurches, but it laid track straight and true. It was constantly fed by a train at the back, feeding rails onto it for laying. It was as revolutionary a development for aboveground work as the Lewis Bar was for tunneling work.

"Yup. Two more machines invented by or for the railroads to make the job more efficient. At the same time they make life easier and safer for the working man."

For some reason Cam had a flash about a woman he knew. In the past she was a firebrand agitator. Old Ella Queue would have disagreed with him. She would have said the only reason the machines got invented was so greedy bosses and owners could squeeze more profits out of the poor working crews. Like most people, he understood that profit was a factor, but that worker safety was important too.

A colorful comment illustrated his idea. "Whether you're a gandy dancer or a rock man, either of those machines makes for a safer, better job."

Mik had his own ideas about machines in the workplace. By and large he agreed. "Yes. You know elegant isn't a word usually applied to this kind of work. But the Lewis Bar is in fact elegant. It addresses and solves several problems in one swoop. It helps stabilize the face and overhead work surface, and makes it easy to keep the work area clean and uncluttered. The whole thing may be stylish at least to your typical rock man. Even so, quiet, it is not. The tunnel work face sites are noisier than a catfight in a thunderstorm."

Taking a mouthful of coffee, quietly, Mik finished his thoughts on the din of the tunnel. "The air drills running off of compressors, trains coming in empty going out filled with muck, the sounds of rock being loaded into the cars, timbers being stood up and braced, the occasional dynamite blast, scores of men working, talking, swearing, all add up. Like I say, noisier than cats fighting in a thunderstorm."

Smirking, Cam cupped his hand to his ear and looked Mik in the eye. "Did you say something?"

Mik silently mouthed words at him, words he wouldn't use at the dinner table.

Cam laughed, nodding. "You got that right. If you want a refined, quiet workplace, you'd better become a librarian. I do have to say, though, those muck trains are cute with their dainty two foot gauge, aren't they? The locomotives may be electric powered, but they still make plenty of noise. Can you imagine if they had to be steam powered, what a hellhole that place would be?"

Mik looked his friend over like he'd just spit in the soup. "Cute? Have you gone soft, Cam? They're smaller than the standard gauge we'll run when the tunnel is done, yeah. But that engine running on two foot track is still plenty of machine. Don't get in the way of one. They're small enough to work in the area. And they are a good way to haul the muck out. Better than man or mule powered ore car. Or steam power, like you say."

Cam chuckled. "Just kidding. Those little extra narrow gauge trains are doing good work in there." He paused. "It is early 1927, Mik. It has been years, and finally this crazy tunnel is getting towards done! The front faces of the pilot bore are approaching each other, soon will be fifty yards or less apart. They'll hole through pretty soon. And the main bore won't be far behind."

"Yes, those crews are close enough to be shaking hands. It'll happen soon."

The friends did a high five.

"In a year or so they'll be running regular trains under the mountain!"

DOWN IN TOWN, SUCH DETAILS WEREN'T IMPORTANT. NO ONE cared about two foot gauge muck trains, or noise, or the Lewis Bar. They liked to hear about progress on the tunnel, the main points of it but not the gritty details. Otherwise, life trudged on.

Ella spent much of her time helping Dale with his business. Her doubts about private business were deeply held and remained just below the surface. She saw the advantage of business harnessing enlightened self interest. She just wanted more emphasis on enlightened and less on self. That a business was run to meet the needs of the customer not the employees had never ever occurred to her.

At heart she was a labor agitator and all around activist. Childhood at the bottom of the economic and social pile bred in her empathy for the powerless. She never forgot how it felt to be on the outside looking in. That said, she first made sure she was taken care of. She also loved poking a thumb in the eye of 'management,' her shorthand for those who had made the climb and needed little help.

Lately she had adopted another foundling, a helpless thing being taken advantage of. The Colorado River.

"That river has run for millions of years Dale. Look at what it has created and sustained without our interference."

"Yes, E, it has been around practically forever. It has a rhythm, like you say. Year in and year out, it gets big in the spring with snowmelt. That extra flow is how it carves canyons and moves boulders. The flow, the amount of water it carries, ebbs through the summer and fall, sleeping in the winter. And then the cycle starts over. It is perfectly balanced. How can anyone look at that and think there is no higher power running things?"

She raised an eyebrow. "Well now that is a different question entirely, and is one we can't solve easily. The river, now, I agree, the river has run perfectly for more seasons than I can imagine. But now, we humans are interfering."

"Interfering how?" He mimed taking a drink. "The few swallows we take out of that river will never be missed."

"A few swallows? We are taking more than just a few swallows. We're taking gulps, more and bigger gulps. Now we divert part of that spring runoff, from near the headwaters, and move it to lakes and reservoirs for our own later use. That means we—the leaders and people of Colorado—are making the river permanently smaller. Do we really understand the effects of those changes? What about the deer and fish and willow trees and beavers? We are starving them of water!"

His eyes rolled before he could stop them. Oh no, here we go down another rabbit hole, he thought.

"Dale! Don't you roll your eyes! This is important!"

He just couldn't get excited about the deer and trout. Hell, they wouldn't even miss the water. If they didn't get eaten first.

"Ella. We're not taking about that much. There's plenty of water out there. Do trout need water more than kids need it? People need to be healthy too. And who is to say that a human drinking water is any worse than an elk drinking it?"

"Well, I'm hearing rumors. They are trickling everywhere."

She smiled at her play on words, waiting for him to get it. He didn't.

"Rumors about what?"

"The rumors are trickling, get it? Water! We're talking about water."

He rolled his eyes again, smiling and groaning.

She giggled, then calmed. "The rumors are about the city of Denver and their grabby water engineers. They are fixing to seize the river and darn near strangle it."

"How so?"

"The old Denver Union Water Company used to provide water to the citizens of Denver, right? Come to think of it, David Moffat was an owner of that company. He owned a large part of it as I remember. That's neither here nor there." She shrugged and forged ahead.

"The thing is, about ten years ago it was sold lock stock and barrel by the private owners. The City bought and re-formed it as the Denver Water Board. Most of what Denver acquired was pipelines, treatment plants, and so forth. Denver Union's water rights were part of the bargain too. This is a big thing, Dale. They—the Water Board—got substantial rights to water from almost every tributary to the upper Colorado River."

"Lot of good that did. I bet that most of it still runs down to California and Mexico."

"Bear with me. They own the water—all or most of it—flowing in the Blue, Snake, Ten Mile and other rivers up near Breckenridge and Dillon. And they own rights in the Williams Fork range southeast of there. And like you say, up till now they had to watch all that water flow out of state. But not for long."

He was catching on. "The tunnel?"

She nodded. "The pilot bore. The Water Board is looking to lease the pilot bore after the tunnel is done. They'll use it to move water from the upper Colorado to the Denver basin."

He jumped in. "You know, I heard Gerald Hughes was involved in the planning for the tunnel. He was a big gun in the old Denver Union Water and stayed involved with the Water Board. When the Moffat Tunnel Commission was formed he pushed for building a pilot tunnel alongside the main bore. He talked it up. There were some good reasons to put through a pilot bore—check out the geology, give access to all points of the working tunnel, and so forth. But why did an old water buffalo insert himself into the building of a railroad tunnel? I wondered about that, and I wasn't alone. Lots of folks were curious why he should he care about it."

"What does a water buffalo have to do with it?"

Dale laughed. "A water buffalo is a term for a water engineer or lawyer or ditch rider or other person involved in the use and transmission of water, and the trading of water rights. Hughes is a water buffalo if anyone is."

She got to her point. "I'll bet Hughes had that—leasing the pilot to carry Denver's water—in mind from the start. He had a way to get his water diversion and he found a way to get it without having to pay for it!"

She looked triumphantly at him, like he should applaud her logic. He didn't. So she went on. "I'm sure of it. And those are the kind of people I'm worried about. They will suck the river dry if they get a chance."

"Well, Ella, I don't know what we can do about it. Except buy land now, on the edges of town."

"And we'll see more of that. People moving in, building, using water….Where will it end?"

"And that, my dear, is exactly what the Arapahoe and Ute Indians asked each other when a bunch of white men came over the horizon in 1859. You can't stop progress, Ella."

XI

CHARI WAS THINKING, THINKING, TALKING. THOSE TWO activities didn't always occur together but today they did.

"This room is nice now. The furnace works well to keep it warm in the cold seasons. But come summer...it will be hot. I wonder if the weather will be warmer than usual next summer? Seems like things are getting hotter overall, at least I think so." Charity pulled out a handkerchief and pretended to wipe her brow. She made a show of not doing it daintily. She wanted Joe's attention, and grumbled on.

"They can keep meat and produce cold in a railroad car, right? And food cold in a refrigerator. So why can't they keep people cool inside of buildings?"

"Good question, Chari. You're right. A refrigerated railroad car is no bigger than a few rooms." He stood and pushed the window further open. "Maybe this will let in a breeze. Matter of fact, I was reading the other day about a man named Willis Carrier."

"A man, huh? Men run everything. I'm sick of it."

Joe ignored the irritable remark. "Carrier has invented what he calls 'air conditioning.' It is a system to cool a room like a furnace heats it. I guess he has been at it off and on for years. It is what, 1927? He came out with his first version in

1902, and an improved one in 1912. I understand the machine has been getting more efficient and reliable since. We should look into it. Even if a man did invent it."

The smile in his voice made her look up.

"I still say if women ran things we'd be better off."

"Don't be too sure, C. Things would still be cockeyed, just a different version of cockeyed. For example, I saw in the paper that last winter a woman bought a seat on the New York Stock Exchange. First one. Did she cause a new, just, warm and feeling era on the financial scene? Did she set all those greedy selfish men straight? No, it is business as usual. I'll bet she is getting rich like the men, but has made no other changes."

She ignored the jab. "You and your news. Here's some news, important to Denver and us, and I'm surprised that you didn't mention it. The pilot bore of the railroad tunnel has holed through! The mountain is finally giving way. That is good, don't you think? The job is getting done! But...." Here she paused, searching for words.

He stepped in. "But what? I'm glad it is progressing, and Colorado's northwestern residents will have better rail service. Plus, it was my deal that got the tunnel financed, and I am glad it has worked out."

"That is the thing, Joe. The tunnel is about finished and its financing will be finalized. New bond sales will plummet— few new bonds will be floated. And soon, none will be needed. I guess I can't complain. The job started with predicted costs of about six million dollars. Last I saw, the total cost was up past twenty three million dollars. And counting...."

A lascivious leer lit her face, followed by a mope. "I got my share of the bonds. And now I need to find another source of income. You know, Joe, I really think that IRC will take off. We can make a mint. Its time to start recruiting."

He shook his head. "Nah, not yet."

"Yeah, we should. That $100 we invested down near El Paso turned into much more. Imagine if we make it a big effort. If you don't want to start building, I will. I'll go find some folks on my own. We need someone to do the day to day work.

He should have known this was not just idle talk. Since he was still focused on the railroad and the coming tunnel he only half heard her. It was a moment he would come to remember. His response was absent minded at best.

"Well, alright, do what you think is needed."

Then Joe changed the subject back to the big news. He wanted to talk more about the crews meeting under the mountain.

"And I knew about it, the holing through, yes. The crews met, joining up the east and west pilot bores two or three months back. February 18 1927, to be exact. It is amazing to me that they met pretty much dead on. The two ends started over six miles apart and dug blindly for years. At the meet, the tunnels were off only eighteen inches horizontally and about forty inches vertically. That is really accurate work, isn't it?"

He looked at her, now fully focused on the topic. "Damn, the surveyors who told them where to dig should get a big bonus for that!"

Chari was thinking on her tasks for her scheme. Since he didn't seem real interested in it, she figured she would keep him talking. That would buy her time to scope things out and arrange them in her mind.

"So when do the trains start rolling?"

"Oh not for quite a while yet. It is only the pilot bore we're talking about here. First the main bore needs to be holed through and done. There will be much to be done yet. Finish the grade, take the construction machinery and works out, lay track, wire the signals, test it all…. Plenty of work yet. To answer your question, I'd say it will be next winter, February or March of '28. At least a year yet.

WATER WAS ALWAYS A TOUCHY SUBJECT. DALE AND ELLA finally agreed to disagree. No point in arguing about the life of a River, or about sending some of it through a tunnel to Denver. There was nothing they could do about it anyway. So they just didn't bring it up. No need to; the headlines of the day provided plenty of other subjects to discuss.

Ella started asking questions.

"Why are the British invading Shanghai? They say it is to 'protect British investments.'" She shuddered. "Now why are a few buildings and warehouses full of stuff worth a soldier's life? I just don't understand. I mean, really, what are they doing, sending armed men clear around the world? Why should they stick their noses in there?"

Dale knew why but didn't attempt to explain. He also knew she wouldn't accept the answer or the reasoning, and that she would just ask more questions. So he merely humphed a muttered response, and sidled around the subject. Aviation was in the news. He loved it, it was technical and sporty and glamourous and so twentieth century!

"And how about that Lindbergh fellow, Lucky Lindy they call him! This spring, flying from New York to Paris, alone, in a tiny one engine aeroplane. Talk about a brave man. He had to prop his eyes open, flying with one hand, for a while, just to stay awake. Thirty three hours, takeoff to landing. Wow! Clear across the Atlantic! Now he is a hero. Has a parade in his honor wherever he goes. I tell you, the world is moving so fast now. Planes across the seas, telephone conversations across continents, the new railroad tunnel nearly open now...."

Troops in China forgotten, Ella nodded. "Yes. Events are moving fast. Seems to me that distances are shrinking. Not literally of course, but practically. For example, that tunnel will save a full day to get to western Colorado. That is a day people can put to other uses. Workers can spend time with family instead of slaving on the job, for example."

"Yup. Everyone can be more, what's the new word? Productive?"

She barely heard him. "And electrical wonders! Last winter, when the pilot bore holed through, was quite a show. President Coolidge back in Washington DC, two thousand miles away, threw a switch. And that switch set off a blast inside the mountain here in Colorado. And the last barrier between the bores fell, and it opened the tunnel."

She stopped then went off on another toot, against the big guys taking credit for small guys' work. "It isn't fair, the President getting that glory. What did he do to earn it? He should have stepped back. The rock workers, the rockmen who ran the drills and loaded the muck into cars and did all the other tasks should have gotten that honor. They're the ones who put in long hours and saw friends killed and waded in floods and got dirty. I'll bet they wanted to set off that blast early and steal the politicians' thunder!"

Little did she know that a group of workers tried and almost got away with doing exactly that. They were stopped the night before the ceremony. Dale was glad and sad about that. On one hand, he was glad he didn't have to explain to the Governor and President how his men had done it. On the other, had they managed to take matters into their hands, it would have been a fun story for the history books. The headlines would have been something!

She went on. "Anyway, even if the wrong man threw the switch, it was an amazing show of technical knowhow and savvy."

"Yes, telegraph wires can carry all sorts of messages."

"And when Coolidge threw the switch, you were there, Dale. How did you wangle an invitation?"

"Well, I do know a few folks here and there."

He feigned shy humility, but was secretly pleased and proud to have been included.

"The ceremony was late February, the 18th as I recall. I heard the crews actually holed through a few days earlier, the 12th. The west crews got bragging rights. The two groups were not far apart, close enough to hear the other drilling. The west's drill bit hit air and they shoved a rod through to be sure. The east crewmen tried to grab it and pull it through but couldn't. It was quite a tussle I'm sure."

He grinned at the image of crews pulling and tugging on a one inch steel rod, two or three thousand feet below the top of the mountain.

"Anyway, on the 18th. Old 'Silent Cal' sat in the White House and threw that switch. That closed a circuit and it allowed the electricity out here to set off the dynamite to demolish the wall between the crews. There was a crowd, and as the boom subsided they rushed forward from both sides. Good thing the roof didn't drop on the onlookers!"

He paused, thinking of what could have been. She was thinking the same. "Thank God for that. On top of the other deaths that would have been a big jinx."

Dale went on. "That can happen, delayed rockfall after a blast. Anyway….All the top hats were there. Our Governor Adams was on the east like I was. He and the mayor of Salt Lake City, Mr. Nelson, shook hands across the rubble. It was quite a scene. Newspapermen were taking photos and a newsreel crew tried to get film. And this was only the pilot bore, the teeny tunnel too small to carry a train." He was tiptoeing around the water aspect of the pilot bore, and tried to rescue himself. "It's not even the main part of the show."

He was too late. Mention of the pilot tunnel set Ella off. "Ah yes, the pilot bore. The one that will steal water from the Colorado River and send it to thirsty real estate tycoons in Denver. Maybe it is too bad there wasn't a big rockfall, big enough to choke it out. Take a few politicians with it, good for us all."

He smiled empathetically. "That wouldn't have been good, especially for me. Ella, we may as well use that tunnel for something. It is too small for any vehicles or such. Besides, we're guessing about it carrying water. All is rumor. Nothing has been agreed to nor money changed hands to move water through it."

"I still hate it, and I hope it never happens." She paused. "The main bore holed through a few weeks ago, no? June 27th? No fanfare then, was there?"

"No. It was old news even as it happened. It will take the crews—mine and others'—months to make it a real railroad tunnel. It will be next winter or even spring before it is in shape to be used."

THE CREWS THOUGHT BOTH OF THE HOLING THROUGHS WERE A big deal. They cared more about it than the typical city dweller. After all, they were the ones who had spent the past years of their lives working to get to that point.

A shift foreman on the east side was describing what it was like to Cam and Mik.

"We could hear the west crews hammering and moving. It was uncanny, like just a house wall or a sheet between us, sound moving back and forth. Of course we were each trying to get the first drill bit through into the other side's air. They got one through first. We grabbed the pole they shoved over, trying to pull it away. Couldn't. We had eight or ten men but they must have had twenty holding on to it. So they won the honors."

"Right now that is a big thing. In six months, who will know?

Mik nodded, agreeing with Cam. "And who will care? That was just the pilot bore. Now, the main tunnel is holed too, and no one even knows who got their bit through first. The thing is, the tunnel is almost done!"

"I agree." Cam continued. "We have a big long hole. The bore does go all the way under the mountain. But there is lots to do. Now it needs to be finished up—smoothed, shored, old machinery out and new track laid, signal wiring, ventilation…. There is work aplenty for lots of folks. It will be eight or nine months, maybe a year before trains run regularly."

"How long will they keep the pass open, our road over the Hill?"

"The rails will stay for now, for a season or two. But the pass won't be kept open. The rotary plows will be brought down, Corona Station will be closed up, and the snowdrifts will again rule. Unless something in the tunnel goes very bad in a big way, the tracks over the Hill will be pulled up. I give it two or three years at most."

Suddenly Mik and Cam were each overcome with memories. The two men were barely aware of the room around them, of the foreman watching. Each was awash in their own private histories and events recalled. Images of scraping or blasting grade and laying rail up and over the continental divide mixed with recalled glee, terror, and gratitude. Herds of sheep grazing on top of the pass in green summer growth covered the land. There were cold fireboxes in stranded engines, spur of the moment adaptations, snow and cold and glare and smoke and cinders and wind, derailments, snowslides, stranded passengers, sending a load of freight up behind a plow.... Creating and running the road over Rollins Pass was a watershed life experience for them, for every man and woman involved.

"A chapter of history and our lives is closing, even as chapters on the tunnel start to be written. I am most grateful to have been part of the great Rollins Pass road adventure."

Cam looked his friend in the eye. "I couldn't have said it better myself."

CHARI TALKED TO HERSELF. NOT ALWAYS, BUT, FRANKLY, often. It helped her organize her mind, her priorities, things in general. She wanted to sort out her future.

On a personal level, as far as she could tell, she and Joe were doing well. Things were good. They saw eye to eye on the important issues, and knew when to give each other space. It was the finances she had to get her head around. They were flush now and had plenty of income.

She sipped a cup of tea. And thought, and talked. The tunnel and the Pueblo levees were finishing up and the income stream from the bonds would stop. She needed a plan or plans. Had to consider alternatives. Especially she wanted to talk through the IRC deal. Joe was out somewhere so she was alone. Well, the cat was there, but as usual was asleep. So the only being to hear her ramblings was a potted geranium. Chari found it a good listener. She stood, holding the tea cup.

"First we need a steady supply of IRC certificates. We can find someone to go to Mexico and buy them. For that matter, keep an eye on Canada and Cuba. They're close and might be a good source. And we need to keep a finger on the pulse of other countries and their currencies. It will all depend on currency fluctuation, of course."

She wandered the room as she talked, setting down the teacup and blankly looking at it before picking at some yellowing geranium leaves.

"And. And, we need to go find investors to fund the purchases. They well be the guys we pay, be our milk cows. Need to be sure they don't skim under our noses. So, our guy comes back with a bale of IRC coupons or I should say envelopes from Mexico. We take, say, a thousand pesos' worth. Take them to the local US Post Office. We exchange them for US postage stamps. The thousand pesos cost us twenty bucks in El Paso. The stamps we bought with the thousand pesos, twenty dollars, is exchanged for stamps worth fifty two bucks. We pay the milk cows twenty or twenty two and a half. Voila!"

She stopped, grinning, and took the teacup to the sink, filled it with water, and gave the geranium plant a drink. "There, honey, that should make you feel better. You looked parched."

Her grin got even wider. "Maybe we can find a friendly postmaster to expedite our exchanges. For a small remembrance if need be."

Down the street, a church bell rang noon. Lunch time. But Charity was on a roll and eating could wait.

"So, whether we partner up with a postmaster or not, we have the spread, fifty two for twenty. A good width of money to work with. It may change a little bit with each batch, depending on economics. I just love how this works. We can play currencies all day. If the Mexican Peso gets strong against the dollar, we go to some other country. The potential is huge! But what we really need is a stream of people giving us money to invest. Doesn't matter where we buy the IRCs as long as we buy them at the right price. And if we keep money coming in we can ride this tiger a long way."

Hunger finally got her attention. She sliced an apple and cut a smallish slab of cheese. Sitting and munching, she daintily sipped coffee out of that teacup. Still the ideas came. She pulled a Cam, talking around a mouthful of food, the thoughts spilling like hail from the sky.

"If we can double our money, we can pay investors an attractive rate, but not so high as to make people suspicious or greedy. Maybe eighteen or twenty percent. No, too much. Fifteen is good. Even that will attract attention! Like I was thinking, we need folks to invest. And I like the idea of lots of people investing small amounts. That way no one investor has too much clout. We don't want the tail wagging the dog."

Her eyes widened. "Ideally, we have so much money coming in that we can't find enough IRCs to put the money into. Tough problem to have, no?" She chortled to herself. The cat half opened one eye, then returned to the serious business of its nap.

She grabbed the cat, put it in her lap, and stroked it vigorously. The cat, half awake, was at first not amused. The strokes felt so good that the kitty relaxed purred loudly.

"That's it! We hype it up, get lots of people giving us money. Pay as we go once we get it going. And we take the spread, the difference between the one hundred percent gross yield and the fifteen or eighteen we pay out. Literally we take it. Take it to somewhere safe. Manila or Cuba or somewhere, even the stock market in our individual names. We don't leave it in a suitcase under a bed. We take it out of the Sheriff's and everyone else's reach."

Her grip on the cat loosened. It looked up, decided the petting was done, and jumped down. Chari looked at the fur stuck to her fingers from the apple juice and the forceful petting. Distastefully, she walked over to the sink and began cleaning her hands, still talking. "And when the time is right, Joe and I...."

Someone rapped on the door. Chari rinsed and wiped her hands, then looked through the peephole. Ella! Not sure she wanted to face the animal loving business hater, she almost ignored the knock. Then an idea came.

"Hi Ella! Pleasant surprise—I was just thinking of you." The smile in her voice seemed genuine. "How is the animal business?"

"I am not in business."

Chari switched from hearty to sheepish. "Figure of speech, my friend. I know you do a lot of good work looking out for your four footed friends. No offense?"

"No, no offense. I see what you mean. It is just that I'm touchy about business. Chasing profit seems grubby. No offense, Chari, you work for yourself. But companies make me think of owners and managers taking advantage of workers to get a profit. The bigger the company, the worse they treat the very people who get the job done."

Chari saw an opening. "Funny you should say that. From time to time I see that too, and it concerns me." This was a stretch. Charity Hovus was concerned only that she get her commissions when she sold a bond. How that money was used, whether any workers along the way were fairly treated or animals abused, was of no import. She really didn't care. But saying so got Ella to listen.

"Oh really? That surprises me, Chari. Since when?"

"Yes, Ella, really. There is more to life than trampling people to make money. Yes, I have been selling bonds and all. I really believe raising money for projects like the railroad tunnel is worthwhile and goes to good use. But I am moving away from that."

"Oh?" Ella knew that such a simple response often brought a wealth of information. Sometimes the wealth was right there, the question clearly answered. Sometimes it was hidden in what was said and not said, or in how things were said. But the open-endedness of it encouraged people to talk and talk. She expected she'd have to read between the lines this time.

"I, well really Joe and I, are looking at a product. It involves big returns, up to fifteen or so percent. And it is based on government issued documents. So the risk is nonexistent! It is open to small investors, people with twenty to fifty dollars to put in.

Ella stared. Her look communicated her disbelief.

"That sounds awful good, Chari. What is it, part ownership of the Daniels and Fisher tower on Sixteenth Street?"

"No, no, nothing like that." Chari laughed. "Real estate is a good buy, but it won't give you these returns, no way. No, this is nothing like that. Like I said, it is based on government issued instruments."

"Oh?"

"Yes. Government backed. Many of your animal friends could benefit. They need money, don't they?"

Ella was sure there was a hook somewhere in there. She was very cautious of Charity and money. Especially her money, or that of a friend. But small amounts, and government backed? Couldn't hurt to listen, she figured.

"Tell me more."

XII

DALE SCANNED THE PAPER. "I can't believe it is 1928 already, and time to think about another Presidential election. The campaigns have revved up. We hear promises and threats and slurs against the other candidate and so on. It is only summer—it starts earlier and earlier every election year. You can't help but hear speeches and read articles and see newsreels all about Al Smith the Democrat and Herbert Hoover the Republican. They're trying to convince me to vote for them come November. Blah blah blah."

"Well, don't read it if it upsets you."

Ella smiled as she delivered the good natured poke. He teased back.

"Boy oh boy, give women the vote and let a few of them drive, and they get swelled heads. First thing you know they are telling you what to read and think. What's next? Telling us how to vote?"

"Well, someone has to look out for you guys," she bantered. "I agree, it is too early in the season to put up with election blather. Each side blames the other for all that is wrong and takes credit for all that is right and good. You know, they want us to forget the importance of every-day people going about their lives. That, more than their efforts, is what makes this country run well and be safe and strong."

"True that. What a choice the two Parties have given us this year, huh? Out of a hundred million Americans, is this the best they can do? On one side, a New York Catholic big city mayor. As Vice President they offer another New Yorker, an old money playboy. On the other side, a Stanford graduate millionaire. At least he didn't inherit his money. He made it on his own, an orphan made good. But with his millions, he can have no idea about us real people and our daily lives. Good grief! Don't the party bosses realize there is a whole big country between the Hudson River and the Pacific?"

Dale was on a roll. He stood and waved his arm expansively, like gesturing to a crowd. "Things seem to be going pretty well now for us Americans. We're not shipping soldiers off to war somewhere. New things are invented every day, things that make life easier. Anyone who wants to work can find a job."

That reminded him. "Colorado's labor troubles seem to be quieting down. A while back there was a big brouhaha up east of Boulder, by Lafayette. Struggles and labor leaders and deputies at the small coal town of Serene. It was a year or so ago. I'm surprised you didn't go up there Ella. Remember? Marches, fighting, strikes. But that has settled down, with the economy and good prospects."

"My days on the picket line are over, Dale. But the working man is still getting taken advantage of and don't you forget it. Labor unions are down right now, but they will be legal and commonplace, you wait and see."

"Hah. That will be the day this country goes down the drain. But anyway, things are good. Even for your precious 'workers.' Heck, even with Prohibition they can still go out and have fun. New inventions which make life easier are coming out left and right. Washing machines to help with laundry, automobiles that are easy to operate, radios….These are exciting times! Best of all, the stock market is helping a lot of people make serious money. I can't see why we should change things up by voting in the other Party's ticket."

Ella wasn't so sure. She had never voted for anyone but Democrats or Socialists. Even some of them were too business friendly and conservative for her. Still, she had to admit some good things were happening.

"I hear that a woman who a year ago bought a seat on the New York Stock Exchange is now a millionaire. These damn uppity women, now some of us are making more money than men. What is that about?" Grinning, she was happy and relieved to see that he took the joke smiling.

Big money made her think about Chari and Joe's plan. The one Chari said was supposedly backed by government documents. And how the two of them wanted her and Dale to join them.

She had learned about that in a recent visit with Charity. The two of them were over their argument. Neither said it but each just decided not to push their views on the other.

That day Ella wasn't looking for a business opportunity or anything like it. She simply wanted to enlist Chari's help. Ella wanted to have Joe introduce a bill saying women and men must be paid the same wage for the same work. Such a thing seemed only common sense to her. Most every man she mentioned it to didn't see the need for a law, and didn't want the government meddling in how privately owned businesses were run. These were the standard objections to any new law, she knew.

Anyway, she didn't get the chance to propose or even mention it. It never got to where she could ask about the likelihood of Joe's backing. Instead the conversation was about some new investment Chari was boosting. Her enthusiasm made Ella wary. Chari's liking something, especially something around money, was two strikes against it as far as Ella was concerned.

The idea itself, the investment product, seemed strong and on the up and up. But working with those two seemed like reaching into a tub full of snakes. Probably they were mostly garter snakes, slithery but harmless. But what if there were a few rattlers slipping and sliding around in there too? She wasn't crazy about taking that kind of a chance.

After Chari threw out the idea, Ella was curious. "Tell me about it."

Chari gave an appraising look and smiled. She had been working on a file, had it open and spread out. She quickly closed it, gathering the pages and stuffing them in. Ella's years as a labor negotiator gave her experience reading documents from afar. She regularly confronted the bosses in their offices and often got good information by reading papers on their desk. The print was upside down but she quickly learned to glean its meaning anyway. Today she noticed Chari's file had 'I R C' on the tab. She would check on that later, but first wanted to hear what Chari had to say.

"I can sum this program up in a few words: High returns. Government backed coupons. Small investors welcome."

"Sounds awful good, Chari. Maybe too good! But I like the idea of small investors. Explain.'

"Well Ella, what we have is simple. We sell coupons which we bought at a discount."

"How....?"

With a smile, Chari shook her head. "Ah now. That's the secret sauce. I can't tell you how we do it. But we do, and the return to the investor, the investment yield, is double digit. We can pay twelve, even fifteen percent per annum." She paused for effect, than added the kicker. "And we pay quarterly."

She knew the spread she had to work with was quite a bit bigger, but wanted to start low. "So, if your animal shelter puts in fifty, we can return fifty seven and a half dollars. First payment in three months."

Ella confirmed the numbers in her head. "That is a hefty number. Are you sure?"

Chari, nodding, knew her audience. "Imagine how much dog food or animal doctor service you can buy with those returns. For that matter, a Union's retirement fund could sure benefit from this. Or a widow's welfare fund. Think of the families of those six rock men that the roof fell in on."

Ella was skeptical but she was hooked. She had to know more about it. "That sounds…wonderful. Not the rock men of course, the investment. You say it involves government backed coupons?"

"Yes, good old Uncle Sam issues the paper we use to back these returns. And no, I won't—can't—tell you how it works. You can understand, confidential information and all."

"Government backed, huh? Small amounts accepted from investors. Hmmm. Let me talk to Dale about this. You say you and Joe are running this?"

Ella was both excited and repelled. Years back, she and Dale worked an investment scheme with Joe and Chari. Things had not worked out the way they all expected. This time Ella would make sure that didn't happen, no matter what. In any case she wanted to look into this.

Chari liked the sound of that, of Ella talking it over with Dale. She hinted at more. "Yes, Joe and me. If things go the way we think they will, we will need help. Maybe you and Dale? I mean your help to run it, not just investing in it."

She put on a meek look. "I'm sorry, Ella, you came to see me about something. I was inconsiderate and excited. So I jumped right into this coupon scheme. I didn't mean to cut you off. What is on your mind?"

Ella's mind was racing to figure out the 'how to' of such returns. And what was the mention of coupons? What did the prominent 'IRC' on Chari's file mean? She smiled sweetly. "Oh, I had a question for Joe on some legislation. It can wait."

A DAY OR TWO LATER, BACK HOME, DALE WALKED INTO THE room holding a letter and its envelope.

"Hi Ella. I heard from my old friend Casper. Remember him? He's now living in Mexico, a town called, something, I forget." He rustled the letter and read aloud. "He is in Acapulco, on the Pacific coast. Says he loves the sunshine and pineapples, not to mention the senoritas!" He smiled, picturing his friend on a beach.

"And look at this. He wants me to write back about the Tunnel. He even included return postage, an envelope marked 'I R C.' I guess I just take it—it stands for International Reply Coupon—to the postmaster and he'll put postage on my letter. Prepaid. I can use it to reply with no money out of my pocket. Pretty slick, huh? Old Casper must really want to know about the railroads here."

"Let me see that." She grabbed it away, dropping the letter and studying the envelope. She saw the IRC. Bought with

Pesos in Acapulco. To be traded here for dollar denominated postage. She looked into the distance.

"Do you feel well, Ella? You're looking like you see a pot of gold or something."

Ella said nothing, still thinking. Of a sudden, the pieces fell into place. It was quite a trick they were playing. Joe and Chari were working the currency difference!

She absently handed the envelope back, then grinned. "Glad you heard from your pal. He doesn't know, but he gave me the clues to solve a puzzle."

Curious, his fingers waggled with a 'let's have it' motion.

"Chari and Joe are up to their old tricks, Dale. I didn't mention it but she was boosting a scheme the other day. It sounded darn good, too good, and I have been trying to figure it out. I think this is it. Your buddy Casper provided the last piece of information."

"Casper?!"

"Yup. With his prepaid IRC mail. See, when I was there, Chari had a file marked 'IRC.' She shuffled papers in and closed it up quick like she didn't want me to see it. I'm pretty sure she doesn't know I saw it. Then she told me how she and Joe had this plan, backed by the government, small investors welcome. Said she could pay huge returns, fifteen percent. I think this is how they are doing it."

"With Mexican postage?" Dale laughed. "Good one, E."

She ignored the joke. "You know how the dollar is strong against the Peso?"

He nodded. "I guess so. For now, anyway. That changes over time."

"Sure, up today down next month. Anyway, they are riding those waves. I think they are buying coupons in Pesos then converting them to US postage then selling the stamps."

"Well, if you say so. Why do we care?"

"She wants us 'to help them,' she said. Remember the last time they wanted us to 'help'? They brought us in and gave us titles and so forth, and then tried to make it look like we were the movers behind the plan. In fact they tried to leave us holding the bag."

"Yeah, I remember." His voice was flat, his memories of the time gray.

"This time, let's return the favor."

He grinned. The expression reminded her of the crocodile she had seen in a newsreel. "I'd like that. How do you think we ought to get started?"

"We go to Mexico and buy fifty or a hundred dollars' worth of IRCs. No wait! We buy them here, take them to Mexico, and exchange them for Peso denominated coupons. Then bring them back, exchange, and…. Nah, that is too complicated." She puzzled a moment. "We buy them there, bring them here, exchange for US postage, and sell. With the spread—which we should get with the exchange rate—we ought to get a good margin. They're offering to pay fifteen percent to investors, so they are getting more than that. We ought to be able to do this without investors, at least to start."

He pondered her strategy. "Is that what they're doing? Buying, exchanging, using the spread to attract investors?"

"Near as I can tell, yes. I'll try to coax more information out of them."

He was getting into it. "Can we find a way to ride on their coattails? Somehow can we use their purchases to our advantage?"

A fresh set of eyes looking at a problem almost always sees new solutions and angles. Dale's eyes did just that, found a niche. "There can't be but a limited amount of IRC coupons out there. Can we corner the market and then sell to them? At a premium? Without their knowing it is us doing it?"

"Dale Smertz, you are a genius. That way we can get them coming and going!"

"And we can pull the plug any time we want. Let them get into it and extended, then cut them off…."

"I like the sound of that. Even if we don't, just knowing we have that power is delicious."

They looked at each other, minds working furiously.

"Alright E. How about this for a plan? You are already in Chari's confidence or at least she thinks so. So you go ahead and work with her, find out what you can about their plans. Tell her I am not interested right now. Tell her I'm looking into building a railroad tunnel or a dam. Out of town, in Arizona or something. Keep me totally out of the picture. At least until we understand the game."

"And why should I do all the work while you're in Arizona playing at master builder?"

"You won't be and I won't be. See, you will be keeping her soft and thinking she is in the saddle, in control. You spend the time trying to get her ready to buy her coupons wherever she can. Maybe you heard somewhere about some mysterious outfit with access to IRC coupons. Of course, that outfit will be us. In the meantime, I won't be working a project in Arizona. I'll be down there buying up every IRC I can find."

Ella smiled as she edged toward the door. She stopped, turned, and spoke. "Good plan, cowboy. I'll go work on Joe and Chari."

He hugged her, looking into her eyes. "Go get 'em. I will go to El Paso to buy up what I can." And he did.

XIII

A WEEK OR SO LATER, DALE HAD A VALISE FULL OF IRC COUPONS. Southwest Texas and north Mexico were hot, dusty, and sparse. The work was not easy. He hit every post office within two day's ride of El Paso. Since he had wads of cash and stacks of negotiable coupons, caution was the word. He took his pistol and kept a chair propped under the hotel room door. Sleep was patchy as he tried to keep one eye open. There were pickings to be had on both sides of the Rio Grande. He was sure he swept every little town clean. Far as he knew, there were no more prepaid postage coupons to be had.

The last night in El Paso he treated himself to the best hotel in town. The next morning he went to the station and waited. The seats in the train depot were cold and hard. The clock seemed stuck as he sat, willing his train to come in from the north. The station agent said there were no delays and it would arrive on time, which it finally did.

Dale stood as the engine slowly chuntered in belching smoke, steam and noise. Passengers climbed out. Watching them, Dale was reminded of a flock of goats suddenly unpenned. Some stood and looked unsurely around while others knew exactly where they wanted to go and wasted no time getting there.

One of the hesitant goats looked like Joe Eggers. At second glance, it was Joe. What was he doing here, hundreds of miles from home? Then Dale realized he was probably doing the same thing, trying to buy up IRCs.

He walked over and greeted his colleague.

"Well hello Joe. You're a long way from home! What brings you way down Texas way?"

Surprised, Joe took a moment to set his valise down before he extended his hand. "Hello Dale. You're pretty far afield yourself, aren't you?" He glanced appraisingly at Dale and his bulky valise. "Maybe not so far after all. I heard that you are working on another railroad tunnel, one that is down somewhere in this part of the country. Any truth to that rumor?"

It felt good to stand and walk on solid ground after a long train ride, and Joe was happy to see someone he knew. "At least that is what someone told me. How is the project going? Who is it for?"

Glad for the conversation, Dale smiled as he sidestepped the questions. "The work is going pretty well, actually. Things come up and you have to think on your feet, as you know. But all in all, I can't complain. You?"

Joe knew that Chari was trying to entice Ella to join their plan. He didn't know if Dale was in on that or not.

"Oh, I am working with Chari." He looked around to be sure no one was listening. "Actually, Dale, she and Ella are working on an investment program. I'm involved too. Now that the Moffat Tunnel is about done, bond sales are dropping. Your construction crews will be done before long too. The job and its income stream are soon to be a thing of the past. What are your plans? Will you disband your crews or what?"

Dale shrugged. Joe went on.

"This scheme of ours, no this plan—scheme sounds awful flighty—is a good one." He smiled, trying to overcome the mention of 'scheme,' and continued. "It will pay the investor well. Ella knows lots of folks who could benefit. I imagine you do too. Are you involved with Ella in all of this?"

"Ella mentioned she had some plans to work with Chari. Didn't fill me in on specifics. She is excited." This was for Joe's benefit. Ella was excited, alright, but for reasons of her own. "It is just as well that she has this to work on. I'm busy with my projects down here. It looks like I will be tied up for some time. It is hard to tell about that."

Joe was happy with what he had learned from this conversation. Dale knew Ella was involved but he wasn't and probably wouldn't be. That was fine with him. He let it drop.

"Well, I have appointments, so had better get going. Good to see you, Dale. Good luck with your new works!" They shook hands and parted. Dale got on the northbound train. Joe headed for the region's post offices. He anticipated filling a valise with peso denominated IRC coupons.

TEN DAYS OR SO LATER, JOE WAS BACK IN DENVER. IT SURE seemed longer than a week and a half since he left.

He pushed open the door and looked in. Chari was relaxed on the sofa, stroking the cat. She smiled, happy to see him.

"Hello, my special traveler! Glad you are back. We had a record week here. There has been an influx of new money and more people tell us they want to participate. We can sure use those coupons you got down El Paso way."

A deadpan look crossed his face. She thought he was trying not to smile at her good news and at his successful trip. Not so. He held his valise up, opened it, and turned it upside down. One prepaid envelope fluttered out onto Chari's lap. She picked it up the looked up at him, confused and alarmed.

"That is all I could find. One measly reply coupon. In a week! I feels like I rode or drove to every two bit village and town in northern Mexico. God, there are a lot of dusty little post offices there. It feels like I saw more of the country than Cortez did."

Charity had read about Cortez. The early Spanish explorer went all over what is now the southwest US.

Joe stood there, moody. Then he sat down next to her, rubbing his eyes with fatigue and frustration. "There are none to be bought, Chari, literally none. They are cleaned out. Most postmasters just shrugged. One told me some gringo had been in a day or two before and bought him out."

She stared at him. "Is someone else in the hunt too? Do you know who? Any description or anything? Man, woman, short tall? Anything to go on?"

"I tried, but didn't get much. I did ask several postmasters what the person looked like. White guy, nothing really unusual about him, blue maybe brown eyes, didn't speak much Spanish. Good grief, that could be me or almost anyone. Maybe this is just chance. These are small towns out in the middle of nowhere, after all."

"It doesn't sound like chance to me. One post office sold out, sure, that could happen. But every one you visited across the area? No, something is not right. Someone is doing this on purpose. We need to hold off. And we need to find out what the heck is going on. Figure out who that 'gringo' is if we can."

A FEW DAYS LATER, CHARI AND ELLA MET TO DISCUSS THE plan. They had a tense and not particularly pleasant lunch. Chari was out of sorts. Ella acted sympathetic but inside she gloated. She was pretty sure her and Dale's efforts were causing distress.

Ella was detailing her supposed success pushing the product and blithely prattled on.

"I'm finding strong interest for this investment. My union and animal friends, many of them, want to know more. The promised returns get their attention." Ella stabbed and nibbled on a tomato wedge; Chari watched with distaste as her colleague continued. "I am confident that I'll be able to bring you as many small investors as you want. How do you want to handle that? Do we have a brochure or something I can hand out? Or should I start introducing you?"

Chari had little appetite. The salad didn't appeal to her and she just pushed it around the plate. "Don't promise too much, Ella." She made a decision. Ella was pushing harder than expected. So she tapped the brakes. "As a matter of fact I want you to slow down. Don't talk to any other people for a while. We need to put a hold on new customers for now."

"A hold? Why? I am just getting some traction. A hold? Are you sure?"

Chari flared. "Yes, I am sure. I said to hold off. Are you deaf? Don't talk to people for a while."

"But why? I thought this was a done deal." She knew why, but did her best to look uncomfortable. "I have appointments next week, six or eight of them. I can't just not show up."

"Buy some time. Stall. Move them back. The thing is, we are experiencing…difficulties."

"If I start waffling now with these prospects, we'll both have difficulties. What is the matter?"

Chari took a deep breath. Should she tell? Did she want Ella to know? She had to tell someone. It just didn't make sense and it would help to share it.

"The thing is, Ella, a problem has arisen. For some reason, we're having trouble acquiring coupons. They just aren't available now."

"Why not? Isn't the government printing them? Why can't you…"

"We don't know why. We're looking into it. It seems someone else is out buying them up. Who and why we don't know."

"Oh. That can't be good. Is there anything I can do?"

Chari was unhappy. Her face got redder and she felt angrier with Ella's every concern and question. With a serious look, she said, "I told you what to do, Ella. No new activity until I give the all clear." She got up and stalked out without another word.

Ella finished her salad and enjoyed the main course alone. As the dessert came, she mused that they seemed to have guessed right, she and Dale. They nailed what Joe and Chari were up to. And they were able to drive a spike into it. No one knew who was strangling the market, and she intended to keep it that way. Sipping her coffee, she figured they should turn up the pressure.

Later that day, she brought him up to speed on her lunchtime conversation.

"Here it is, Dale. They are perplexed and dead in the water. Chari told me to hold off, not do anything more until she tells me to. She is upset and angry about it. She stomped off before her meal came and left me the bill."

"Did she say someone is out scouring the country and that they can't find any to buy?"

"Yes, they think so. Don't know who, from what she said. I think they are at a loss what to do. So, do we flood the market ourselves or contact them anonymously and offer to sell them coupons?"

"Contact them is the thing to do. Carefully. I'll send a letter. Today." Another crocodile grin.

The knock on the door was faint and at first didn't register. Chari was poring over a stack of checks received. Not bad. If only they had coupons to exchange to generate the cash to pay these people a return.... Joe was filling out a deposit ticket to get them into the bank.

After a minute she heard the insistent knock. She groaned, stood, and opened the door. A boy in uniform held out a clipboard. "I have a packet for Joseph Eggers and Charity Hovus. Please sign here."

She ripped it open. Joe grabbed the letter inside before she could read it. Whatever it said made him speechless and his eyes bulge like a toad's. She took and read the piece of paper.

"Joe, this is outrageous! I can't believe they had it delivered by runner. I wonder just who is this outfit called 'Top Karat Partners.' There are no names of course."

Deep breaths helped him to calm down. Good thing, because she was purple with rage. Joe was afraid she might burst a blood vessel she was so worked up. He reached for the letter but she pulled it away.

"Let me see it again, C. Maybe I can figure who it is from. Or learn what they want…."

"I told you, Top Karat Partners, whoever they are. I don't know, but that is how it is signed." She shook the letter like a terrier shaking a rat, wanting to stun or kill. That was what she would try to do if she could get at the writers.

"They say they know what we are doing with the IRCs. And they want to make a deal."

"What? How…?"

"I don't know how, but…." She held the letter out.

He again scanned it, glancing at her from time to time. With another deep breath, he slowly read it word for word. Then he set it down as if it were fragile.

"This isn't great, Chari, but it could be worse."

"Oh yeah? How? How could it be worse, Joe?"

"They didn't have to tell us about it, could have cut us out altogether, that's how."

He gave her a quizzical look. "So maybe we'd better settle down, Chari. They just want part of the action, that's all. I guess there is enough to go around. Now they want to supply us with IRCs, as many as we need."

With a smile he thought of his days on the train and riding mules, horses, and the occasional car around south of El

Paso. "Actually, that makes it easier for us. We can concentrate on recruiting investors and investing our own spread."

"I don't like it, Joe. We don't know these people. They may well get us into doing business with them then lean on us somehow. They want something else and we don't know what."

"I don't like it either. And you may be right. But right now, seems to me we have little choice. We just have to go ahead as we can, and be real careful. You saw how many coupons I got last trip—a grand miserable total of one. At least this way we can stay in business."

"Now we know something about the 'gringo' who was down there before you."

"I guess. So how do we get in touch with these Top Karat characters? He reread the letter. "It says they'll be in touch. Wonderful. So we wait."

Charity had calmed down. "Well, we're no worse off now than before. Let's hope they contact us soon."

"Are you sure they got the letter, Dale?"

"Yes. Chari signed for it this morning. They're stewing and moaning right now, I expect. I also expect that they'll cave, and wait for us to contact them."

"Stewing and moaning is fine with me, as long as they're the ones doing it. It is good for them, don't you think?"

"Maybe so, for a little while. I hope they don't do too much. That wouldn't be good for us. We don't want them to have time to think it through and plan a way around us. Alright, are you ready for round two?"

He had a photograph of a stack of IRC coupons. That and a sheet of paper went into a large envelope. The paper had instructions how to swap cash for the coupons. A different delivery runner was summoned to take it over for Joe and Chari's pleasure.

"We'll know soon. If they don't buy, we can sell them ourselves, and reap our own returns."

XIV

Another messenger, another envelope. Charity hefted and shook it then held it to her ear and listened. Not that she expected to hear anything, but she wanted to be sure before opening it.

"What, are you hoping it'll tell you what's in there?" Joe impatiently grabbed at the packet.

She pulled it back. "No, I'm just checking."

She opened the clasp and pulled the contents out. If looks could cause paper to burst into flame, ashes would have been floating in seconds. She couldn't take her eyes off the photograph.

"Look at all those coupons. I bet there are hundreds of them. No wonder you couldn't find any."

Her look was part commiserating with Joe, part anger at the sender. "And half a sheet giving us 'payment instructions.' The nerve!"

Joe took it from her, scanning and flipping. "And the instructions are anonymous. No way to tell who is behind this 'Top Karat' group. There is no return address or anything." He held it away and mournfully stared, then threw it down.

"Of all the…! Who in God's name do they think they are? Hogging all those coupons. Those are public property, available to anyone. Who are they to buy them all up?" The irony of complaining that someone beat them to it was lost on him. Not her.

"I have to hand it to him, or them, whoever this Top Karat is. If I stumbled onto a good program, I'd find a way to do the same, muscle in and try to get a piece of it."

Sad and resigned, he shook his head. "I suppose. But I sure don't like it." They exchanged a long look. "Seems to me we have no choice, C. Do we? What else can we do but play along, at least for now? I mean, we have investors lined up to buy. And people to pay."

She nodded. "You're right, that's really the point. Some are waiting for their interest payments. We need coupons to redeem to generate money to pay them."

Pulling a surprise on Joe was hard to do. Shocking him was impossible, or so Chari thought. He acted stunned at this. "You mean you haven't been setting people's interest aside for future payment? No separate fund? Haven't kept proper accounts and records?"

Now it was Chari's turn to be surprised. She figured he was kidding but played along. "Joe, this is a scheme, not a damned mortgage bank. You knew that going in. The plan was, is, to get a flow of income coming in, trap it, and move on. Maybe retire somewhere. We aren't in this to pay our customers more than we have to. Right?"

She gave him a searching look. "You do know this, right, Joe?"

His expression was so sheepish the thought crossed her mind he would not speak, merely give out a 'Baa.' She almost laughed at the image, but did her best to remain stern.

"Yeah, Chari, I know that. This letter surprised and upset me, and I guess I just didn't think before speaking." He laughed. "Of course I understand we are herding sheep in to be trimmed."

There's the sheep again, she thought. This time she unsuccessfully stifled a giggle.

"What's so funny about that, Chari? You are right. It is simple and straightforward. Not always easy, but simple. We give them a little bit of feed for encouragement, that is, pay a dividend or two. And that gets get them to come back for more. Sooner or later they are sheared smooth and we have plenty of our own wool set aside. We put it somewhere safe and at some point, we go away. I get that."

"She smiled, relieved they were pulling the same direction. "For some reason it just struck me funny, Joe. Sheep and shearing and so forth is an image that, well, makes me chuckle. That's all."

He nodded, uncertain at her amusement.

She got down to business. "Well, I think it is time to round up some more sheep and scrounge up more feed."

He smiled and half nodded. "Seriously, let's be practical. We have to make some interest payments soon, right?"

"Dividend payments is how we have called it."

"Dividends then. So, we need to get our hands on these coupons to get them sold and generate some money coming in." Here he picked up and shook the photo of the coupons some anonymous person or persons had sent them.

Chari took the letter and photo. "I will handle it. I'd like to smack this guy's nose, and I will when I meet him."

"Chari, Chari. I know what you mean. I am sure we will get the chance to get back at him. Or her. Or them. But right now, like it or not, we need him. Let's think. Maybe the way to go is to make the payment and exchange, but not in person. We need someone to insulate us from these jokers. When we expose them I don't want any more connection than we already have."

"You're right, Joe, as usual." Chari was prepared for this. "How about Ella?"

"Do you trust her with money and coupons?"

"Yes and no. If we build her up, make her feel important and part of the team and all, she'll go along. And we can offer to toss in a little to her animal fund."

"Animal fund?"

"Heck, I don't know for sure, but I bet she needs money to run her animal welfare schemes. We can say we'll make a contribution after she is done with our job. Or we can lean on her a little if need be."

Chari shrugged. "Anyway, she'll do. Yes, I think it is time for her to step in and help us. Besides, people think she is a purer than snow. No one would suspect her of carrying lots of money or being part of an investment scheme."

"I see. Yes, let's meet. With her, and with Dale, if he's in town. He was working on some project down south. Let's get them both on board if we can. We need errand runners and a public face besides us. Can you set it up?"

Chari dreaded actually having to see Ella. "Alright. I'll try to set something up. How does your schedule look for tomorrow or the day after?"

THE NEXT DAY, THE FOUR MET AT A CAFÉ. DALE SAT AND PUT HIS hands behind his head, stretched, and grunted. It was a feel good sound, not a painful one. He brought his hands down and looked around. Jumping right in, he opened the conversation.

"Thanks for inviting us, you two. It is always fun to catch up with old colleagues over a meal." A big smile lit Dale's face. It could have been sarcastic or genuine. His tone, however, tended to the sarcastic.

Joe glanced at Chari and smiled at the purportedly friendly statement as Dale continued. "Ella and I look forward to hearing about your operation."

Neither he nor Ella let on that they had knew or had surmised what it was about it and how it ran. Nor that they were doing their best to hijack the lion's share of the profits. He asked a basic, innocent question.

"Now, you say it is backed by what? Government paper of some sort? Tell us about it."

The explanations and clarifications took some time. After a while, Dale looked sideways at Ella, seeming to telegraph skepticism. Then he gazed across the table at Charity and Joe. "The thing is, we aren't sure. I am a builder, Ella a…a community leader and organizer. We're not financial people. We are not sure if we should put our names on this. I mean,…."

Ella literally bit her lip when Dale started to talk. The teeth stayed on the lip half a second or so, causing pangs but not drawing blood. Unable to help herself, she interjected.

"He means, why do you need us? This is your deal, your plan. Why not put your names on it? Are the two of you unwilling to put your names out to the public? If so, why should we?"

Ella objected exactly as expected, and Chari had a response ready.

"We want you because you two are well known. And you are respected." Chari didn't really believe that, and had to rehearse to get the disbelief out of her voice. Joe's glance told her he agreed with that. She turned to Dale.

"You, Dale. You built, or had a big hand in building, the Moffat Tunnel. Your company did good work and you treated your men well. That makes you notable, almost famous, here in Denver."

Dale started to smile at the overblown compliment. He snuffed it, partly. After all, it was true that he did a lot of work on it, and that people knew it.

A groupie couldn't have smiled more warmly than Chari did. Dale almost blushed in her rays. She then turned to Ella.

"And Ella Queue is well known as an advocate. Like Dale said, a leader. Everyone knows she is concerned for animals and workers and women. Her heart is truly in it." Chari felt a gag coming but managed to suppress it. "She is known around about as the paragon of upright caring."

Joe tried to smother a laugh. The resulting smile was noticed and appreciated by Ella. Or 'Saint Ella,' as Joe wryly thought. He took over.

"Charity is right. You two are known and respected and you lend us seriousness and a solid reputation." He paused. "We need you. The investors need you. Our suppliers need you."

Ella and Dale both fought not to glance up at the mention of suppliers. Their thoughts at this statement were parallel: 'Darn right the supplier needs us—it is us!'

"Plus, and this is confidential." Chari looked each in the eye and got an acknowledgment. She intended to close the deal, to set the hook and reel them in.

"I agree with Joe. We mean it." She looked at each, smiled and nodded. They seemed to agree.

"Now, like I said, this is confidential. I mentioned something about this to Ella the other day. So, we tell you this for your use only. Now that you are our partners. You are, aren't you?" She didn't give a chance for a response and kept right on talking.

Here Joe spoke up. "The thing is, we are bringing in lots of investors and money is flying around like crazy. But we were having trouble getting coupons. Supply and demand and all that. Anyway, that created a bottleneck, potentially serious. But we're past that problem. We managed to locate a source."

He conveniently omitted that the source located them, not the other way around. Of course there was no mention of the unknown, anonymous letter from some person or group. Of the evidence that they had cornered the market and then coldly dictated terms to Chari and Joe. Ella and Dale of course knew all that. They played along, doing their best to simply nod in wonder at Joe's expert handling of the situation.

Taking their nods as agreement, Chari took up the tale.

"The thing is, we need to keep at arms' length with this source. We know a little about them and vice versa, and we want to keep it that way. That is, they want privacy and we want privacy."

Joe spoke. "So, we need a go-between. You have business experience, we know and have worked with each other, and you are known in the community. We trust each other."

At this it was all Dale could do not to stand up and walk out, but he sat still and didn't change expression.

Joe of course didn't hear these thoughts, and he finished his spiel. "You would be perfect to help us get these coupons. That can be the first job for us, our partnership."

Dale and Ella exchanged glances, brief so as not to burst into laughter. Chari mistook it for concern.

"This will be a straightforward arrangement. No hazard, no funny business, nothing like that. We wouldn't put anyone in a bad situation."

They nodded acceptingly and she went on.

"Tell you what. After the exchange—we'll give you the details and you'll see it is simple—afterwards, we can do some things. Dale, we'll make sure your company's name is on all the printed materials. All the promotional materials for the investors, that is, printed professionally and businesslike. Good advertising, no?" Chari gazed, waiting for Dale's response.

It wouldn't do to seem too easy, he was sure. They had to show at least some reluctance. "That would be good, but who is this so-called source? You say there is no danger. How can we be sure? Why should we—the four of us—work with them?" Dale intentionally used 'we' not 'you,' in effect joining the team. He paused; neither Joe nor Chari responded.

Before they could object, he threw in the towel. "Well, alright, if it will help us—you and us—with the plan, I think we should do it." He looked at Ella. It seemed he was passing the decision to her, but she knew better. She stalled, seeming reluctant, but really hoping one of them would sweeten the pot. This could work out better than they had hoped!

Time to finally close the deal, thought Joe. He locked eyes with Ella. "And Ella, there's another thing we can do. What we can do, and this is up to you, is we can donate some amount of every investment to your animal shelter. Say a tenth of a percent?"

She didn't trust these two. The prospect of a flow of money, even a temporary one, was good. And since it was supposed to be for the animals, she had good reason to agree. Her enthusiasm made Joe think his idea put her over the line.

"That would be nice, Joe." She looked at Chari then Dale before extending her hand to him. "You got yourselves a deal. What do we do now?"

"We'll have you exchange cash for the coupons they have. Here, take this to the address shown. You should get a package of coupons in return. Bring them back as soon as you can." Joe handed an envelope over, with an address on the outside.

"Done. See you later today or tomorrow morning." Dale and Ella left, smiles and handshakes all around.

JOE STOOD, GRINNED, AND DID A LITTLE JIG. "Wow, C, you laid it on with a trowel. 'paragon of upright caring'? Where did you dig that phrase up?"

"It just came to me, Joe. But she bought it. So did he. They bought it all. I suppose paying a tenth of a point to her is a small price to pay."

"Chari, there a Niagara Falls of money coming in. And it grows daily. We have enough to pay them some and the investors some and the animals some and still have a bunch for us. And like you discovered, there aren't enough coupons out there to buy. But still the money comes in."

Her smile drooped to a frown. "Good problem to have, no? Money coming in like crazy? But how can we accommodate new investors?"

It was not a rhetorical question. They had money coming in but no apparent way to finance the dividend payments.

Even if Dale or Ella returned with a valise full of coupons, they would be scrambling. What to do?

Suddenly she knew. The solution hit her like a beanbag.

"Joe. Who needs coupons? That just slows the whole cycle down. Here's what we do: Pay the old investors their dividends like usual. We do it with the money cascading in from the new ones. That works, doesn't it?"

He thought on it for a moment. "Yes! It will work long enough for us to set aside and invest a pile of money. Sooner or later the flow will start to dry up. The trick will be to recognize that point and get out. And that is why it'll be good to have Dale and Ella on board and have them be the public face."

He grinned and held a hand up. She did the same and they had a high five. She too grinned.

"Same old trick. You'd think they might wise up, but I guess not."

His arms snaked out, grabbed, and pulled her close. She loved his boa moments. "Fine with me if they go for it again. Now, how about an old trick for us?"

XV

THE TUNNEL HAD BEEN OPEN FOR MONTHS. WHEN IT OPENED, February 28 1928, it was a big deal. There were speeches, ceremonies, and publicity. Time went by. The tunnel's efficiency and safety were soon old news, taken for granted. People went on with their lives. Dale put the construction business on hold, letting his crews go. Joe was still a lobbyist and consultant at the Capitol. Chari was done selling bonds and focused on her investment strategy. Ella continued her community work. News focused on the good job market and soaring stock prices.

Spring's languorous kiss yielded to summer which sped by. Autumn loomed. Before long, days would shorten and temperatures start to drop. In the newspapers, the Presidential campaign took center stage. The claims, promises, and mud slinging heated up. Herbert Hoover, the Republican candidate, was ahead. Oddsmakers named him to win. Before long Americans would vote, and people could get back to the business of making their own lives better.

CAM AND STEU LIKED TO TALK ON PUBLIC AFFAIRS, THE campaign, the stock market, and other items of current interest. They often met with other retired railroaders for coffee. Sometimes Mik sat in, sometimes not. 'Geezer's Grounds,' they called these confabs.

"Say, that stock market is sure going wild, isn't it? Steu, did you put money into it like you said you were going to?" Cam swirled his coffee cup as he looked at his friend.

"Yes, I have." Steu looked around to be sure he had the floor. "In fact, the doorman at my hotel gave me a hot tip last week. I bought shares of the stock. The price has tripled! So, yes, I am happily in the stock market. I should say, most of my money is in it and I am happy with the results."

Cam stared, took a big mouthful of coffee, and swallowed noisily.

"The doorman…. Great God, Steu. Stock tips from the doorman? What can he know but rumor? Is that wise?"

"Hey, my investment tripled. Can't argue with that! And I can borrow from the broker. He calls it borrowing on margin. He will lend me a portion of the increase in value to buy more. The amount of the loan is dictated by the margin between stock purchase amount and amount it is worth now. It is kind of complicated, but it is really sweet! I'm getting rich!! Lots of folks are doing it. You should too!"

Cam grimaced. "I was going to say, don't put in money you can't afford to lose. But it sounds like I'm too late."

Steu was hooked; money lust had him. He didn't even hear Cam's dour advice.

Others in the group read the financial pages. Most everyone across the country watched developments and some made money at it.

"Speaking of hot tips and big returns, have you heard about the postal coupon scheme?" A retired conductor was a longtime Geezers Grounds member. He chimed in. "It is being promoted by Dale Smertz, the tunnel contractor. You know him, don't you, Cam?"

"Yes and I would be careful. I did some contract engineering consulting for him. That was alright; he seemed to know how to get and listen to good people. He did well managing his part of a big project. But I don't think he knows anything about investing. Recently he approached me about his scheme, or his plan as he calls it. He promises a fifteen or twenty percent return. That doesn't make sense. An honest way to produce those results is beyond me. Like I say, I know him and he was alright as a contractor. But for money? I wouldn't trust him with a nickel."

"Oh really? I think I may put some money into it, give it a try."

Cam snorted. "You guys with your fancy investments and huge returns. You go ahead. What's the old saying? If it seems too good to be true, it probably is."

As he was leaving, Cam decided to look into this postal coupon deal. It didn't feel right. He didn't want to invest, but just to satisfy his curiosity.

LATER, CAM WAS TELLING MIK OF THE MEETING AND ABOUT Steu's fixation on the stock market. Not to mention Dale's scheme. On checking, he had found that Joe and Chari were involved, behind the scene. That got him even more worried.

Mik grinned, frowned, then blustered. "If Joe Eggers

and Charity Hovus are involved, it is not on the up and up." Cam expected Mik to react just this way. Mik didn't stop, but forged right ahead.

"They are using postal coupons? And supposedly have thousands or tens of thousands of investors? Good grief, even if it is legitimate, just how many of those coupons are there? What are they worth? There can't be enough value there to sustain those numbers. And like I say, if Joe and Chari are part of it, grab your wallet because they're trying to get into it!"

Cam nodded. "I agree. And get this, I have an old railroad friend who has put some money in. He asked and I told him I thought that wasn't a good decision, but its his money. Anyway, he gave me some lowdown." Cam paused, gathering and arranging his facts.

"He heard that those two aren't buying more coupons, or very few. They're having trouble getting any. It seems that some mysterious outfit is involved. He says they—the outfit—have cornered the market. Joe and Charity are buying from them. Coupons or certificates or something. Something to back their scheme. He heard the name and I can't remember it because it is kind of. Tockarit or something. Top Carrot, that's it. The owner must be a gardener! It is Top Carrot Partners, I am pretty sure."

Mik walked to the phone. He cranked it and spoke to a friend who had access to licensing records. He asked about the backing of 'Top Carrot.'

His wolfish grin when he hung up told Cam whatever he learned was good.

"Cam, you won't believe. The outfit selling the documents to back their sky high returns, to Joe and Charity?

That 'Top Karat Partners'? By the way, it isn't carrot like the vegetable, but karat like in gold purity." His grin faded.

"So, Top Karat Partners is owned by, get this: Dale Smertz and Ella Queue. Our old railroad and diamond mine schemers. But aren't they also publicly involved in the scheme? What is going on there, I wonder? Weren't those four in cahoots at one time? And there was a falling out as I remember. Well, I wonder if they know something we don't?"

Cam laughed. "Let me get this straight. On one hand we have Joe and Chari kiting returns from a limited supply of postal coupons, supposedly getting their investors crazy big returns. Emphasis on supposedly. And they are running it to the public with an outfit allegedly headed up by Dale and Ella. Now, on the other hand, unbeknownst to them, Dale and Ella are working behind their backs. They, Ella and Dale, are selling them some kind of maybe bogus certificates to back the scheme. And I'll bet they are selling those documents at a premium."

"You may have it right, Cam. You know that Dale character, don't you? If you get a chance, ask him about this, would you? I just hope none of our friends get hurt with this."

"I will." He smirked. "Maybe he will give us a deal on his red hot certificates. Come to think of it, I think I'll try to check the whole thing out. But I don't want to alert Smertz or the others."

DALE LOOKED FORWARD TO THE UPCOMING LABOR DAY HOLIDAY. Late summer weather was exquisite. Plus Ella was always in a good mood because the holiday celebrated the working man. And working women, as she often reminded him, and it had done so since 1894. She would want to watch the downtown parade, which was fine with him.

He had just a few things to get done at work this day. The construction office was closed, the job done and run off. Now he concentrated on investments, on the postal coupon plan. Reading over a list of figures, he frowned. "Ella, look at this. Month before last, investors put in many many dollars, just over one hundred thousand. Last month, it fell by a bit. And this month it lags a bit more."

"Oh. Well, we are having trouble finding IRCs to buy. There just aren't many available. We've even put out offers in Central America and Canada. Without the coupons they can't pay interest."

"That's part of the problem I guess."

She had an idea. "You say money is coming in, right? Why don't we just pay interest to the old note holders with the new money coming in? Skip the coupon steps?"

"But still keep Joe and Charity on the program of buying from Top Karat, right?"

"Yeah. We can give them some sort of a 'coupon of coupons' or some such document. Any official looking piece of paper will do the trick. They'll pay. Even so, maybe we need more people out canvassing for new investors."

"Why? We don't have coupons."

"We need investors to put up cash. We have got to keep money coming in to pay dividends to senior investors. Not to mention the newcomers. The field is limitless. We just need to keep it rolling."

Joe loved summer. The season brought to mind fat of the land, milk and honey, tall clover, and other luxurious expressions and clichés. At least Joe thought of summer that way. Ripe living there for the picking, so to speak. And he was happy that this summer in particular was obese. Their scheme was going great guns and he had big plans for living off of it.

"Chari, look at these numbers. New money was down month before last, and last...."

The interruption of a knock on the door kind of irritated him.

"What do you want?!"

The delivery boy shrunk back, holding out an envelope. "Letter for Mr. and Mrs. Eggers."

Joe knew Chari would be peeved at that. She grabbed it away, turning her back and opening it, muttering.

"I'm not Mrs. Eggers. I am Charity Hovus." Dale and Ella knew this and addressed the letter that way just to irritate them both. After the delivery boy left she read out part of the letter.

"Its from the yayhoos at Top Karat. They are streamlining, they say."

"Streamlining. That's a phrase I haven't heard. Probably, I guess, it means making things more efficient." Joe reached for a dictionary to check. Chari ignored him.

"It says they won't be sending IRCs any more. Instead they will send us 'a coupon of coupons.' They say we can sell it to our investors same as an individual IRC. They say it is as valid as an IRC, backed by them. This way they don't have to send us individual coupons. So they say this will save both them and us the headache of keeping track of thousands of small coupons."

She stopped, looked out the window a moment then at Joe. "I'm not so sure, but if that is what they give us that is what we will use, I guess."

He frowned. "Well, that is a new one on me. But I agree. If we hold it out as a worthy investment, our people will lap it up. It reminds me of cats in a creamery."

Changing directions, he mused aloud, "We had better tell Dale and Ella about this. They are the ones who will have to present this change to the folks in the street."

"Funny you should mention them. Ella telephoned saying she and Dale wanted to talk. No hurry, in the next few days or a week, she said."

They looked at each other then he looked into the distance, thinking.

He was about to speak his thoughts. She was thinking the same things and beat him to it.

"It is time. The money inflow has probably peaked. We need to gloss that over, reassure them. Call it a seasonal lag, the farmers are too busy harvesting to worry about finance, point out it is a normal pattern, whatever it takes to keep them calm. And that this new super coupon is a good deal. We'll even need to buy another shipment of them to put weight behind that. We need for them to keep involved and out making at least some money come in."

"Yup. But it is time for us to plan for, to think about making an exit."

XVI

FALL'S MELANCHOLY RHYTHM WAS BEING REHEARSED. LISTENING carefully, one could hear it behind the background of city noise. Leaves weren't dropping yet. Glimpses of yellow foliage meant the trees would be bare before long.

The change of season couldn't come soon enough for Cam. He liked autumn's clear skies, crisp chill, and the haze of burning leaves.

Fingers curled around his favorite coffee cup, he mused on the season. The mug was nearly empty. Grounds swirled thick on the bottom, forming an aromatic and granular sludge. He looked at his friends Mik and Steu. Then he brought the mug up and guzzled. He recalled doing so many times up atop the Continental Divide, and said so.

"Man, these dregs are like chewing sand. Reminds me of the coffee we used to put up with up at Corona. Like when we were snowed in atop Rollins Pass. For some reason it is the little things like that which I remember. Not the wind gusts wailing away, or snow up to the eaves. That is kind of vague background. What I remember is the taste, smell and feel of coffee grounds. Sure there were big snows and bigger winds, but what sticks are the small things, quiet card games and thick coffee after a day of fighting the storm. "

"Those days are gone, Cam. I doubt there will ever be another card game played at that station. That part of the world has changed, even if the java down here is pretty much the same." Mik smiled wistfully. "End of the line."

He poured himself a cup of the heavily grounded coffee. "You know, don't you, that the Denver and Salt Lake Railway has shut it down? The Pass, I mean. A few trains ran over it last spring and summer, just to check on things. But they have relied on the tunnel exclusively, for running traffic. They didn't even keep the tracks plowed last winter."

"Yes, the winter of 28–29. I watched for that. Only a few maintenance runs went up and over. And those you could count on one hand. I talked to one of the firemen. Conditions up there are about what you'd expect. Things have deteriorated in just one year. If they want to reopen it even for summer tourism, it will take time and money." Cam the railroad man was always watching expenses.

Mik continued. "Corona Station was not manned for the first time last winter. Here it is late 1929. For almost twenty five years, not a day went by that people weren't living at that station. Now it is a lonely old maid, living on memories of suitors calling and glory past."

Cam snorted with laughter, spraying coffee. "Old maid? Suitors? What, are you a poet now?"

Mik grinned. "Nah. It makes me feel a little blue is all. We had some tremendous times up there, didn't we? Built and ran tracks up and over the highest through railroad in North America, we did. And we moved tons of freight and thousands of people. It is sad to see a good set of rails being abandoned is all. Like I said, we are witnessing the end of an era."

Steu nodded. "It is bittersweet isn't it? The Tunnel is open. It is working as hoped, maybe even better. The traffic reliably runs through it. Engines pull cars under the storms. They avoid the weather and problems of running over the top of the mountain. It has shredded the time to run from Rollinsville to Fraser. It used to take eight or so hours on a good day. Now it takes less than one, and every day is a good day."

Cam agreed. "Things are doing well, trains on time and all. People in northwest Colorado and in Denver for that matter are better off for it. More commerce is moving faster and more reliably. Folks throughout the state are seeing benefits from it. Even those in Pueblo, I expect."

A paperboy came into the café, his bag full of the afternoon edition. "Extra! Extra! Stock market at all time highs! Invest now! President praises the good times, promises more of the same! Buy your paper now, only five cents!" He waved a paper, stopping from table to table for those who wanted to buy one.

Steu considered buying one but didn't. His investments were doing well and he was happy with his broker. Turning back to Rollins Pass, he smiled, remembering winters, as Cam talked more about the Pass and the Tunnel.

"Yeah, and there are plenty of other benefits of the tunnel. No more snow slides, at least none that will cut service. No derailments from ice buildup. No more passengers stranded atop the continental divide or frostbite or digging snow drifts down to twelve feet deep so a rotary plow could bite into them. I helped build the road, but its useful life is over. We should move on. In a way it is too bad, but you can't stop time."

Steu continued. "But it is kind of sad to see the line we built no longer needed and the rails rusting for lack of use. I agree with Mik, it really is the end of an era. Sure, that is a cliché but the tunnel truly brought an ending. No more trains running up and over the highest pass on the continent."

Mik grinned. "Listen to us. We sound like a bunch of old codgers. I always imagined my grandparents having this kind of conversation, not me."

Cam nodded halfheartedly. He was on to a new subject. "Yes, building that Tunnel was quite an engineering job." Cam spoke from experience. Not only did he consult on this tunnel. His career was studded with successful drilling. For thirty years, he worked on and supervised the building of scores of railroad tunnels. "Back in '23, crews started six miles apart and bored towards each other. They overcame a huge range of rock conditions, cave ins, floods, oozing walls, what have you."

Mik looked at his friend. "You saw it all, didn't you, Cam?"

"Pretty much. And that was just the trials and problems underground."

"It is just as well that old David Moffat didn't live to see it." Now Steu was on a toot. "I mean, there were financial shenanigans and planning missteps. Really, I should say lack of planning in some ways. There were things done and not done that he wouldn't have stood for. At first, he had to be spinning in his grave. Now it is done and all. He is, God rest his soul, probably long last at peace. This is Mister Moffat's Opus." He mispronounced the word.

Cam spit a mouthful of coffee around a laugh. "What is an ah-poose? Sounds like a papoose! What on earth is it?"

Mik stifled a laugh. "It is pronounced 'OH-pus,' not ahpoose. Opus. What, Steu, you and I are poets now, I guess. At least Cam says so!" He smiled to ease the dig.

Steu looked injured. "I thought long and hard on that line. An opus…" here he pronounced it correctly. "An Opus is a masterwork. Just because David Moffat didn't live to see it, it is still the crown of his long and storied career. If he hadn't done all the railroad and financial work he did the tunnel would never have been built."

Mik ignored this aside. He wanted to talk on the items that went into Steu's 'Opus.' So he held up one finger then two and so on.

He took one fact or situation after another, numbering it as he explained.

"To start with, the bedrock of the whole thing, is that it took a natural disaster—Pueblo's flood—to shake political will and financing loose in order to enable this tunnel construction project." Since he had the floor he continued.

"Firstly, the chief construction engineer assumed, didn't have it checked but just announced, that the rock the west end crews would dig through was solid. Which it most certainly was not and the crews had to deal with loose and fragmented conditions for a long way.

Secondly, the Moffat Tunnel Commission blithely announced they would cover all costs. They built no incentives for cost saving or efficiency into the contracts." He looked at Cam. "I bet your man Dale Smertz loved that."

"Not my man, just an associate who paid for my engineering opinions. And you didn't hear it here, but he paid a lot of 'consulting fees' for peoples' goodwill. And sometimes for certain people to just look the other way."

"Gee," Steu asked, "Did money change hands quietly and out of public view?"

"Perhaps...." Cam smiled knowingly.

Waiting patiently for his chance, Mik resumed his litany. "Thirdly, initial cost estimates of six million or so dollars were ludicrously wrong. By a country mile, actually several country miles. The total cost ballooned to over twenty three million. A four hundred percent margin of error, but who is counting?"

"Fourthly, the D&SL started running freight through it two weeks before it was turned over to them, and didn't pay for it."

"Fifthly, after that, they—Denver and Salt Lake Railway which is a private corporation—got effective ownership of a major tunnel built with public money. They finagled it for a song, leaving the taxpaying citizens of the Tunnel District to pay the bonds off."

"Sixthly," and here he put his other hand up, finger extended. "Sixthly, the Denver Water people got a trans-mountain water diversion tunnel built at no cost to them—the pilot bore."

Cam. "I can't disagree with you guys about most of that. But, still, look at how the northwest part of the State is already growing and benefitting from timely and reliable train service. If I were a young man, I would invest over there."

Mik looked earnest. "It would be a good use of your money, a good long term investment. We have boom times now, like the paperboy said. But remember, booms come and go."

He looked his friend in the eye. Cam felt like the man was looking through into his soul.

Steu jumped in. "As I said, at the outset David Moffat had to be spinning in his grave. Now that you lay out those misdeeds and shenanigans, maybe he's mostly at peace, but does a slow roll now and then. Still, the Tunnel is Mister Moffat's Opus."

Still looking very solemn, Mik spoke from the heart. "Well, it is getting to be time for me to leave. It has been one heck of a run. I am glad to have shared it with you guys. Good bye." He shook hands with Steu, then Cam. Straightening his shoulders, he walked out of the room, intent on reclaiming his life.

Cam found the penetrating look and the formal leave taking a little out of character. Mik usually said a simple, "See you later." Still, he didn't give it much thought. He figured he would see his friend in the next day or two.

Steu looked after Mik. "That almost felt like he is preparing to go away for a while." He shrugged. "Just my imagination I'm sure. Where would he go, anyway?"

"I imagine so, Steu. Probably headed out on one of his mysterious month long trips. Plus, I think he is just having trouble with the abandonment of Corona Station and Rollins Pass."

Steu was determinedly optimistic. "I can't spend my time looking back. Today is wonderful, and the future is exciting! President Hoover tells us we will have good times as far ahead as he can see. The stock market is growing very well and many people have jobs. By all indications, prospects are bright. I will consider investing in northwest Colorado if the right deal comes along."

Here he paused, thinking, smiling. "But, really, you know that most of my money is in stocks and bonds. My broker is in full contact with the New York Stock Exchange by telegram. He phones them almost every day, and he says I should put in as much of my money as I can."

His face lit up. "Say, I got a good tip this morning. So I hurried in and bought a hundred shares. The price has almost doubled already. Easy pickings!"

Cam, skeptical, poured another cup of coffee. "Tell me, Steu, what is the company's name? What does it make or do?"

"I don't remember the name off hand. What do they do? No idea. It doesn't matter if they make marshmallows or wooden legs. I don't care. The thing is, their stock is going through the roof!"

A chill gripped Cam. It was like a cold wet blanket dropped onto his shoulders. Not usually one to pay attention to premonitions, he tried to shake it off. "I hope the suits know what they are doing, friend. And that they are telling us the truth. I hope your money in stocks is safe and you can get it when you need it. Not for me. Playing the stocks is too loosey goosey for my taste."

He got up and paced. This whole stock market with people investing crazily on the strength of rumors and tips somehow made him queasy. "Me, I do a little business with the bank, no more than I have to. For some reason I just don't trust money men. Most of what the wife and I have is kept safe where only she and I can get at it."

Steu didn't really hear this. He was running totals in his head, counting the increase in value of his stock holdings.

XVII

ACROSS TOWN, OTHERS TOO CONSIDERED THEIR FINANCES AND their futures.

Charity looked at Joe who returned the gaze. "The plan is in good shape. IRC's have turned out well for us. Don't you think, Joe?"

He nodded and she smirked.

"At least our part of it is in good shape. The yields and fees, the ones we're keeping, are substantial.

"Yes, they have been rolling in. I want to keep some handy, liquid as it were. Most should go to stocks and bonds, or a solid out of town bank. I like that idea—the stock market is becoming overheated if you ask me."

"Oh Joe, we have discussed this and talked it over and kicked it around until it is bruised and bloody. You agreed with me after all that: We invest our money in the stock market. And it is a good decision. That money is building and compounding like crazy. They are going great guns. Here it is almost October and year to date, the money we've put in to stocks has more than doubled."

She paused, now grinning, and hugged him. "Havana here we come!"

He halfheartedly nodded. "I guess you're right, C. It looks good for us. And, for now, things are going alright for the investors as well. We back our dividends with coupons or certificates from Top Karat when we can. But as we have talked, we have to adapt. Most of what we pay out now is not truly dividend money. It is from cash flow, new money coming in."

He looked warily around the room although he knew they were alone. "Not that I'd admit that to anyone but you, Charity dear."

Her eyes were bright. "I agree, Joseph Dear. Remember, the investors don't care nor would they be bothered if we told them that. People just want their dividends."

"That may be, C, that may be. Anyhow, the question is, how long can we keep it up? At some point we'll run low on new investors and their cash. Before that time we need to be ready to scramble. Because when that happens, it'll be 'Katie bar the door'!

"You're probably right, Joe. Let's just make plans. I say we aim to be out of town by mid month. Halloween night, 1929 at the latest."

"I am getting a little nervous, but yeah, I like Halloween. Let's shoot for that! That should give us time to get things arranged. We can exit with the ghosts and goblins…."

He opened a folder and scanned the first page. "Dale and Ella are on board, aren't they? There needs to be someone to hold the fort or be around to answer questions when we pull back."

"Yes, people like to have someone to see and complain to. And like we decided, we need someone well known to answer questions and keep things smooth after we're out of the picture. They'll do that just fine."

He figured she had it right. "Yeah, the last thing we need is someone chasing after us before we're settled somewhere."

Charity. "I want to look Ella in the eye when we see them. Not that we'll tell them we're planning to fade out of the picture. Or that they get to face investors who feel let down. Not to mention the sheriff. Still, I want to be sure she knows what to expect. I'll set up a meeting."

DALE LOOKED AT ELLA. SHE GLEEFULLY LOOKED AROUND THE room before meeting his eyes. The main thing she saw was a footlocker, a nondescript wooden box with metal shields on the corners. It had a hasp and was securely lockable. Sizewise, it was probably three feet long, eighteen inches wide, and a foot or so deep. Probably it was an army surplus foot locker, used by some anonymous doughboy back in the Great War.

She didn't care about the stories it could tell of sea voyages, barracks, or muddy trenches. She just cared about its contents. It was full of IRC coupons. She and Dale had amassed them 'for future use.' The plan was to keep the locker with them. Maybe they would leave town, maybe they would stay in Colorado. After all, it had treated them well over the years. Either way, soon. It would all happen when the wool over the eyes of Charity and Joe's investors was yanked back.

"I think it is about time to act, Dale. We've gotten money and the investors are getting their money and Joe and Chari are starting to act a little squirrelly. It is about time to pull the curtain back, don't you think? They've paid us thousands, Joe and Chari have, for coupons and certificates from Top Karat."

"Yup, and we've put those thousands to good work. I'm glad we got those dollars into the market. Good to get in on the stock boom. The money from Chari and Joe via Top Karat is most of what we have put in. And the dividends Joe and Chari pay us help. They make those payments in order to keep us sweet. Our money has doubled or more back at the good old New York Stock Exchange. We are in tall clover!"

She thought. "I wonder how they are keeping their dividend promises to investors. We've scoured the country and there are almost no new IRCs out there. So it has to be hard for them to keep up the dividend payments to their investors."

She kicked lightly at the foot locker. "Of course we have a few IRCs here, for our own use. But that is another story…."

"They're probably paying dividends by scamming the new investors. It isn't complicated: bills need paid, use the money coming in. That is what I'd do in their place. It works like a charm." He smiled at that.

"Dale Smertz! How you talk! You would do such a thing? Take money paid to you in good faith and use it for yourself? I'm shocked, shocked and dreadfully appalled." This she said with a faux grimace.

"Yeah, right. As if you would do anything different." He grinned like a hungry man sitting down to Thanksgiving.

"Think about it, E. That is pretty much what we plan to do to those two. Some investors may get hurt along the way. That's too bad, but, well, it is a big bad world out there…."

She grinned, acknowledging. "So now Chari takes the new money and pays the old investors. But of course first she pays herself."

The grin turned to a frown. "Now we know why they wanted us to be involved in the plan. Sure, we'll make a little money, but when it goes poof…! They want us to end up holding the bag. We get to answer the questions and try to make payments. And, for all they care, to meet the sheriff and explain it all to him."

He said nothing to this, merely nodding. She pushed for action. "My sense is, their house of cards is starting to shake. Time to go give it a good push." She pantomimed shoving something over as she finished her thought.

"I want to go look Miz Chari in the eye. I want to tell her—them—that their little game is up. We know how they are using the investors and what they're getting out of it. And we see what they're trying to do to us. And then I want to tell them we are Top Karat."

"Ella, I get that you want to make these two squirm. But let's not get carried away. I don't think we should tell them about us and Top Karat. Having a company like it, up and running, may be useful for us in the future. At least we want to keep the name active and clean. Plus knowing what they don't will give us leverage. We can always tell them later."

As if he hadn't spoken, she went on. "And I want to blow the whistle on them. After I tell her, I want to go to the sheriff."

He stood up and held his hands out, as if to stop someone running at him. "E! Whoa! Think about that. I mean telling the sheriff. First of all, they'll just say their scheme was so successful it got out of hand, that they didn't mean any harm."

"Maybe they have their lines rehearsed, you may be right."

He glanced in agreement, hands still up. "Plus, Top Karat is a legitimate firm. Remember, we sold certificates that were simply made up. I mean, we printed them ourselves. And sold them for big money...."

He sat down. "John Law would take a dim view of that. We don't need them to know what we've been doing. I agree we want to shine a light on Chari and Joe's deal, yes. But we need to keep our skirts clean."

"Maybe you're right." Ella felt as deflated as she sounded. She didn't feel well anyway. Must have been something she ate or drank. She forced bile back down her throat and reluctantly agreed.

"You're right, Dale. We don't want to give them anything to throw at us." She thought a moment. "Anyway, let's meet. We have plenty to tell those two."

AT THE MEETING THE NEXT DAY, SURPRISES AND MORE WERE IN store for the four unlikely business partners. Joe and Chari, Dale and Ella had items they wanted to talk on. Chari started.

"Joe and I have discussed things and we need you two to…."

Dale brusquely interrupted. "Wait, Chari. We need to say something." With this interruption he seized the floor. He looked them each in the eye. "Ella and I know."

Joe chuckled. "You know what, Dale?"

Dale drew a breath. Ella was still not feeling well and hoped she could keep her meal down. She needed to take her mind off her nausea but mostly she wanted to throw lightning bolts. Holstering her tongue proved impossible and she jumped in.

"We know how your fancy investments work. The scheme is carried by currency differences of the postal coupons. Who figured that angle? It is actually a sound and legal strategy, very creative. That is all well and good." The words were harsh like a crow's caw: loud, shrill, elemental and almost guttural. Ella spoke faster and faster.

"We also know you two can't get more coupons. Not at a cheap or reasonable price. We know you are buying them from someone who has cornered the market and is charging you confiscatory prices. We know you are now paying dividends to your first investors with the cash from new investors, not yields or reserves. We know…" Here she stood up to put her face very close to Chari's. "We know you are paying yourselves big money. And we know you want us here to be in charge while you take your money and slip away!"

The volume of voice grew with this list and she positively brayed the last accusation.

Joe was taken aback. This tirade was completely unexpected. He tried to calm her and buy time. "Ella, sit down." He gently took her elbow and guided her to a chair. "Now, what are you talking about, taking new cash to pay old dividends?"

She regarded him with eyes glowing and suspicious. "Your words, not ours, Joe. We know what is happening. No one else does. Yet." She glanced around meaningfully.

"Is that a threat, Ella?" Joe's tone was low and carried its own menace.

Chari was outraged and unable to speak for a moment. Then she couldn't help but spew.

"Oh, you act so innocent and pure, Ella Queue. Supposedly helping animals and 'the poor workingman.' What a charade!" Her anger trumped fact and she blurted an unproven suspicion. "I know most of the money you raise does not go to four footed beings, but to you."

Dale too got a scolding. "And you too, mister bribe payer. I know you paid Joe money to keep quiet and to steer regulators away while you worked on the tunnel. Other people might be interested to know about that and other payments, too!"

She glared. "You two make me sick! You were ready to help and be part of the deal while our plan was going well. And you were happy to take the big money we paid you. Now we hit a hard spot and you are ready to blab to the world. Some loyalty!"

"Loyalty? You talk about loyalty? Charity, you and Joe are ready to leave town with bags full of money. Other peoples' money, given to you in good faith. And you try to persuade us to stick around and answer questions without telling us you're leaving? And you accuse us?"

Ella had backed up a step or two and was restraining herself from launching at Chari. They glared at each other and Joe stood, maybe to get between them, maybe to protect his girl.

Dale slapped the table he was sitting at. It sounded like a rifle shot.

"Alright, I've heard enough." He stood, motioning the others to sit.

He ran through a number of items and facts. As he did he moved his forearm, a conductor using one arm. With each forward movement he put up fingers, counting.

"One. You guys...." He nodded at Joe and Chari. "You guys devised a good investment scheme, got it off the ground."

"Two, it got big fast. Not sure if it just grew like mold on an apple or if you two meant to make a killing. Doesn't matter."

"Three, someone got the scent and horned in."

Here he carefully did not mention the name or that he and Ella both knew a whole lot about that horning in. He tested the waters. "Who is that anyway? Who is selling you the coupons at high prices?"

With unexpected candor Chari blurted, "Top Karat Partners. Whoever that is."

Dale continued as if he hadn't heard, mostly because he did not want to react.

"Four, whoever horned in—this top cart guy—apparently got most or at least a substantial cut of the money."

"Five, you could have been honest with us and the investors. Expenses outran legitimate income. That happens. So, you could have folded it all up, but instead you kept taking money from new investors. They thought they'd get dividends based on your 'government backed' coupons. Instead you used their money to pay yourselves and the early investors."

He raised the other arm and index finger, "Six, because of this, instead of an investment gone bad, you have provided fodder to the sheriff. He could move in and take action."

He dropped his arms but kept his fingers splayed and looked around the room. "You two have a problem."

Now Joe stood, nodding to Dale to sit. His arms gestured like Dale's had.

"Not so fast. You two need to listen up." The glare in his eyes could have ignited wallpaper.

"Seven. You, Dale, and you, Ella, knowingly participated. You agreed to be part of the scheme even though you knew the risks. You knew or should have known how we were paying for things."

"Eight, you took money you knew or should have known wasn't from dividends but was from new cash."

"Nine. You too have actions to answer for." He sat.

No one spoke as they looked at each other.

Ella's stomach was churning. She tried to speak. Instead, a loud hoary burp came out of her mouth. She silently managed to swallow the burning acid came up with it.

Without thinking, Chari reacted. "My sentiments exactly."

For a second or two, silence. Chari giggled. Dale chuckled. Then Joe roared. Ella too gave a laugh, gassy then full throated. As one person settled down someone else would start a teehee, setting off another round of tension relieving glee.

Finally things got quiet. They still looked at one another.

Joe broke the silence. "Well. Problems aplenty, no?" He half expected another nervous giggle, but none occurred. He was thinking furiously.

"We each have difficulties. Enough that there is nothing to gain by accusing the others. Doing so now makes no sense." He looked stonily at Ella. "Even if the accusations are just."

Ella started to speak but all she could get out was another belched croak.

Chari looked at Dale. "What are you feeding this poor woman?"

He tried to think of a quick, smart retort. He failed; the best he could do was a fairly weak rebuttal to Joe's statement. "Yes, Joe, the accusations you have heard are just."

Dale then stood and paced. "What we have is a standoff. Checkmate. We both have grounds to call the sheriff in on the others. But I agree with Joe. That makes no sense. It is the last thing anybody wants to do. We're in hot water enough, no reason to turn up the heat."

Joe relaxed back into his chair, looking at and gauging his companions. He spoke.

"It is simple when you get down to it. We have money set aside. No doubt you have some saved away too. Here's what we do: get out of town. You go your way, we'll go ours."

Chari didn't like it. "But what about the money coming in like Niagara Falls? Why let that go to waste? At least let's find another person to stick around."

Joe shook his head, glancing at Dale then Ella. "And how long would it take to bring that person current? And where can you find a patsy?"

Ella glanced with hostility at Chari with that. "A patsy, huh?" She paused, then went on. "If you bring some one in it is just one more way the money has to be split. Why make complications? For potentially smaller share for each of us?"

Her voice was a little hoarse but she made herself understood, and it came clearer as she went on.

"Not for a second do I trust either of you. You'd sell me or Dale out in a flash."

"As if you wouldn't betray us more than you already have!" Chari was seeing stars, she was so upset and angry.

Ella ignored her. "I say we split the new money you have on hand today, October 15, 1929. Then, like Joe says, we go our own ways. Let whatever comes in after now just sit in the post office, unopened."

Chari turned a darker red. "And why should we split the new funds with you? You have done nothing but cause problems!"

Dale interjected. "Because we have you in a headlock. Granted, you have us there too. The point is, none of us can get out of it nor let the other go. The only way is to split the money and go away. At an agreed time, like Ella said. Neither of us wants to have the sheriff called in."

He looked intently at Chari. "Or maybe you do…?"

XVIII

"That didn't go the way I thought it would." Joe reviewed the previous several hours. The meeting with Ella and Dale was supposed to be straightforward and simple. Purpose, prep them to be the main operators, get them completely comfortable with being the face of the plan. Of course there was to be no mention that he and Chari would fade out and disappear.

"No, it didn't." Chari sat heavily, and looked as flabbergasted as he felt. Angry but unable to decide who to blame, her mind wandered into possible outcomes. She fell into her 'talk out loud' mode, trying to piece together what had happened.

"So Dale and Ella, the master builder and his girl, miss animal loving pure faced priss, somehow got ahead of us. I'm not sure how but they knew that we are using IRCs to finance our scheme. I sure never told anyone. Did you, Joe?"

He flared. "What an insult! No, Chari, I didn't blab to anyone. You know damn well I didn't. But they knew how we were financing it, with those postal coupons. They also somehow knew about that Top Karat bunch of yahoos who horned in on us. How did that happen? That outfit sure bollixed it up for us. They made things so bad that we had to go to using new cash to pay old bills. Thanks to them we couldn't get coupons to sell to finance the dividends. And now we have to let it fall apart."

"Wrong, bucko." She flared. "We had to pay them, Top Karat, outrageous prices for coupons because we couldn't get any on our own. And that took up much of our profit. Why did you agree to that?"

"Me!? This whole scheme was your idea. We were already in knee deep when they appeared. What could we do then? Heck, you yourself agreed that we had no choice but to deal with them! I'm as mad and perplexed as you are. But you better not try to blame me, Charity Hovus."

Across town, Dale and Ella discussed the same meeting. "That didn't go the way I thought it would."

"No, it didn't. I expected we'd tell them what we knew about their investment plan. Just let them stew a bit, and leave." Ella was aggravated that she didn't have a chance to rub Chari's nose in it.

Not aggravated but elated, Dale grinned. "At least they mentioned Top Karat. Shows how shook up they were, to reveal that name to us. They acted like it was a big secret. Like this big evil company was jacking them around and we should be sympathetic. Maybe we should even cut our percentage of the take since more had to be paid out to Top Karat. As if! It was all I could do not to laugh. We really threw a wrench in the works with that."

Enjoying the small victory, his smiled faded quickly. "Of course they wriggled on the hook. They tried to turn the whole scene around. All of a sudden, they were the good guys, pure innocent business folk. And you and I, because we took their dividends, were the ones defrauding investors. What a crock! Joe even threatened to turn us in. I don't believe he was ready to go to the sheriff, but he sure threatened to."

"And you just sat there, Dale. And took it." She glared at him.

"So what should I have done? Smacked him? I sure wanted to, believe me. Then he would have called the cops, and we'd really be in the soup. I know you felt sick, but you didn't have any ideas at the time, did you, Ella?"

So, each couple found themselves licking their wounds as they readied a quick exit. All four of them were thankful, actually. They were grateful for the money and the timing. Here it was mid October, 1929. Each was very glad to have the chance to go somewhere and enjoy the new found dirty riches.

It was a good thing, each of them believed, that their money was safe and secure in the stock market.

Headlines, *New York Times*

October 29 1929
STOCK PRICES SLUMP $14,000,000,000
IN NATIONWIDE STAMPEDE TO UNLOAD;
PREMIER ISSUES HARD HIT;
UNEXPECTED TORRENT OF LIQUIDATION
AGAIN ROCKS MARKET

October 30:
STOCKS COLLAPSE IN 16,410,030 SHARE DAY

Afterword

THIS STORY IS SET IN THE 1920'S, A TIME OF FERMENT AND change as the Nation came of age. The events and news items discussed all occurred.

Pueblo Colorado and surrounding towns suffered catastrophic floods in June 1921. Several day's rain was followed by cloudbursts upstream. A wall of water surged through the city and on down the valley of the Arkansas River. People along the river from near Canon City downstream all the way to La Junta and Lamar suffered heavy loss of life and widespread destruction.

At a 1922 Special Session of the State Legislature, lawmakers passed a Bill which Governor Shoup signed into law. It enabled the issuing of bonds for flood control and repairing storm damage. The same Legislation enabled the sale of bonds to finance construction of a railroad tunnel west of Denver.

Work on the tunnel started in 1923. It was formally opened February 28 1928. The geology and hydrology of the area were not studied and quite a few unpleasant surprises were uncovered as the job progressed. Ultimate dollar cost was about four times the original estimate. Some twenty four men lost their lives in the effort. The tunnel ultimately proved beneficial to towns along the railroad and to the State as a whole.

The stock market went wild in the late twenties. Manipulation, rumors, and a boom mentality made the heights gained seem impressive. They also made the ultimate financial correction deep and difficult. The Great Depression lasted well into the 1930's.

About that time, there was in fact an investment program based on the sale and use of International Postal Reply Coupons. A man, first name of Charles, figured how to use the currency differentials to make a profit. At first he simply made a good living for himself. Then he brought others in. The scheme grew big, fast. Before long money coming in was being used to pay old investors. Of course it didn't take long to run out of new investors and the deal collapsed.

The man's name is forever attached to dodgy pyramid schemes. Joe and Charity's plan would today be recognized and called a 'Ponzi Scheme.'

About the Author

STAN MOORE IS A HUSBAND, FATHER, GRANDFATHER; A THIRD generation Coloradan; an author and historian; a Vietnam veteran; a retired small business owner; and an avid mountaineer, backpacker and desert rat. Moore and his wife make their home near Denver with two cats who let them stay there.

www.ingramcontent.com/pod-product-compliance
Lightning Source LLC
Chambersburg PA
CBHW021313020526
44118CB00047B/639